# ENGLISH CATHOLIC POETS
Chaucer to Dryden

STATE COLLEGE
CAPITAL OUTLAY PROGRAM

... Elbridge Colby ...

# English Catholic Poets

Chaucer

to

Dryden

*Essay Index Reprint Series*

 BOOKS FOR LIBRARIES PRESS
FREEPORT, NEW YORK

Framingham State College
Framingham, Massachusetts

First Published 1936
Reprinted 1967

INTERNATIONAL STANDARD BOOK NUMBER:
0-8369-0321-8

LIBRARY OF CONGRESS CATALOG CARD NUMBER:
67-28733

PRINTED IN THE UNITED STATES OF AMERICA
BY
NEW WORLD BOOK MANUFACTURING CO., INC.
HALLANDALE, FLORIDA 33009

*To*
MARGARET E. COLBY

# Preface by the General Editor

THE world-wide interest created by the Catholic Literary Revival cannot be confined within the bounds of contemporary Catholic letters. It must reach back into the past and explore its own golden heritage of the ages.

Dr. Colby's book is a notable adventure in this direction. It opens up a large demesne of Catholic poetry, extending from Chaucer, the morning star of English song, to the literary ruler whose period is rightly named for him, "the Age of Dryden." In all this stretch of time, Catholic poets hold no ignoble place. It is well, therefore, that they should be here assembled in a specifically Catholic literary study.

Still other names than those listed in this volume could evidently be suggested for inclusion. But we must bear in mind the author's purpose, to restrict himself to those poets whose rank as English classics can be questioned by no one. If, on the other hand, certain names occur whose presence at first glance may seem unwarranted, the explanation can readily be given.

The first name, perhaps, which might thus be challenged is that of Shakespeare. Yet, it is in no way the author's purpose to reopen the mooted question of Shakespeare's Catholicism. His aim is purely an impartial study of the poet's attitude toward things and persons Catholic.

That Shakespeare was not a Catholic has never, of course, been proved. That he was in actual communion with the

Church of his fathers has repeatedly been asserted, but never established to the satisfaction of the general reader, Catholic or otherwise. That he was well informed and well disposed in regard to matters Catholic seems indisputably true, in spite of certain passages duly discussed in this volume. That, in fine, positive evidence exists, sufficient for building up at least a legitimate hypothesis for his Catholicism, is equally obvious. If more be discovered later more can then be cheerfully claimed.

Another name which likely might provoke a lifting of the eyebrows is that of Marlowe, a Titan in a Titanic age, a poet if ever such was born, a man of genius whose forehead struck the stars, although his feet may often have stuck in the mire. He met the fate he courted. We need not here accept the stories, true or false, that quickly came to be woven about his name. But whatever early connection with Catholicism he may once have had, he certainly became associated with that atheistic fellowship which could not fail to obscure his vision and drag him to the earth. And yet, strangely enough, what concerns us here is the profoundly Catholic lesson which constitutes the central theme of his three great tragedies to which this book refers, and which rightly might be called a Trilogy of "the Heavy Wrath of God." They all deal with the retribution due to sin, which God can defer to the hereafter for its full execution, but which the poet must in some way or other exact upon the stage. In this, as the author brilliantly shows, therefore, Marlowe did not err, though he made his own life the supreme tragedy.

With Ben Jonson's religious affiliations we are more intimately acquainted. Certainly, he could not be over-

## Preface by the General Editor

looked in this volume. Nor, is it difficult to surmise what must have been the nature of his Catholicism, the while it lasted. How truly did he ever grasp, or how genuinely understand it? One greatly wonders. Religiously, "rare Ben Jonson" may not have been so uncommon a phenomenon.

Finally, the last name calling for a word of additional comment is that of D'Avenant. In the full splendor of his reputation, he far outshone his stern Puritan contemporary, Milton, who by comparison, was a quite insignificant luminary that paled its ineffectual light before him in the popular estimation. Times go by turns, as Southwell tells us, and during life it was decidedly D'Avenant's turn and not Milton's. D'Avenant has widely been regarded as a Catholic. While he may well enough have professed the Faith for a period of time at least, yet the question of his religion is not too clear. His continued presence in the entourage of a Catholic queen certainly rendered him suspect, at an early date, as a "Popish dog and curre of Rome," but his poetry itself is less convincing on this point.

With the exception, then, of these four names, whose presence is thus accounted for, all others selected for special mention in this volume, are those of writers unquestionably Catholic. For many of the Renaissance poets, connection with the persecuted faith they had faithfully adhered to from infancy, or had bravely embraced in ripened manhood, implied heroic sacrifice. It meant voluntary banishment for Crashaw, and for Southwell inhuman imprisonment, rack and torment of every kind, with bloody execution at the end in open sight of a gaping crowd, like Christ on Calvary.

After Chaucer and Langland, all the writers mentioned

here are Tudor and Stuart poets. Beginning, therefore, with the first breaking dawn of our modern English literature, we pass through the entire range of its Renaissance poetry so far as Catholics were concerned. To have thus distinctively covered this field is surely a worthy service rendered to English literature. Dr. Colby's work, moreover, is genial and sympathetic throughout, and has been accomplished in a true literary vein.

Little, it may be remarked, is said in this volume of the objectionable features frequently found in the dramatic literature of the entire Renaissance period. While a reference, at least, to this fact is imperative, it is not the scope of the book to enter into its discussion. The book, in brief, is offered as complementing in part the previous volume in the Science and Culture Series, *The Catholic Literary Revival*. From Newman and Chesterton, we now hark back to Chaucer and Dryden, kin with them, observing how all have quaffed from the selfsame fountain their fairest inspiration.

The author of this book, Dr. Elbridge Colby, is himself a convert, as Newman and Chesterton had been. He was three times Proudfit Fellow in Letters at Columbia, where he was accorded his Doctorate in English, in 1922. He was also engaged in teaching this same subject successively at Columbia and at the University of Minnesota. Since his entrance into military service, which has raised him to the rank of Major, he has never abandoned his interest in books and study. His contributions have appeared not solely in military magazines but in the *English Journal, American Speech, Modern Language Notes, Publications of the Modern Language Association of America, Harper's, Current*

*Preface by the General Editor* xiii

*History*, and the like, as well as in standard reference works. In the Catholic fields his articles have been welcomed by outstanding publications, from the scholarly *American Catholic Quarterly Review* of earlier days to our newest comers, such as *Thought*. His volume on *The Profession of Arms*, published in 1924, was singled out by the London *Times* as being then "the best on its subject in recent years," while his *American Militarism*, issued just a decade later, was heartily approved by professional men. This very limited statement may perhaps sufficiently serve the purpose of introducing the author. He has rendered in this book his most distinctive service to the Catholic Literary Revival.

JOSEPH HUSSLEIN, S.J., PH.D.,
*General Editor, Science and Culture Series*

St. Louis University,
May 26, 1936

# Author's Preface

THIS VOLUME has grown out of an attempt by a student of English literature to record the noteworthy Catholic elements found in a reading of those early authors whose writings are universally accepted as part of the canon of classic English letters. The history of that literature has been too exclusively written, the biographies of those men too generally penned, by persons unsympathetic toward the faith which inspired Southwell and sustained Dryden. To us these are not merely great English poets; they are also Catholic poets. Their writings do more than mirror their times; they also reflect their feelings on matters close to their hearts and ours. If we seem to cling too persistently to the Tupper interpretation of Chaucer, despite some criticisms directed against it in the past, we need only say that it seems more faithfully to interpret Chaucer as a Catholic poet, however much he frequently falls short of the ideal which this should imply. We have, therefore, confidently accepted it. If, however, we seem to emphasize too much the religious beliefs of these writers, we can reply that it is our purpose, soberly adopted, to compensate for lack of emphasis here in the common history, survey, or commentary on writers who wrote when all, most, or much of England was Catholic.

The statement of this, which we believe should be the normal Catholic point of view toward these writers, will be found fairly heavily supported with documentary citations and references. It may be true in other realms, as the gentle Vicar of Wakefield once remarked, that "that virtue which requires to be ever guarded is scarce worth the sentinel." Yet it is not true in scholarly fields where the use of the footnote will be found quite common. My earnest hope is that my policy in this regard will compensate in strength for what damage it does in the way of distraction. For those who care not for the so-called scholarly apparatus of annotation and quotation, I can only cite in defense the excellent remarks which Robert Ward, historian of *The Law of Nations in Europe,* included in his preface as long ago as 1795:

"The reader will no doubt observe that I have not been sparing in quotations, both in the body of the Treatises, and in the Notes. I am aware myself, how this interrupts the attention, and particularly how it interferes with uniformity by the necessary change of style. But in an inquiry of this kind it was perhaps unavoidable. Many parts of it are purely critical, and therefore argumentative; and in these cases we know how little an author's word can, or ought to be taken. . . . As I profess not to write for those who read for pure amusement, I have had no scruple in interweaving these proofs and illustrations so closely with the body of the work, that the one is made to depend upon the other for its very connection and uniformity. And I have chosen this mode the rather in preference to appendices, because, as I pretend to no attractions of arrangement or style, I am sensible that the merit (if any) of the following pages, must depend simply upon the faithfulness and accuracy with which authorities are quoted. I am therefore not deterred

## Author's Preface

by the fear of interrupting the course of the narrative, or of diverting the reader's attention. I know not indeed if I am right, but I have long thought that the art of bringing plain and authentic documents into a clear point of view, so as to affirm or deny a thing, or to prove that it cannot be either affirmed or denied, is the great merit of historical or of argumentative writing. Too great an attention to the decorations of language, may often lead us far from this true point. It may please, but without the other it cannot fill the mind; it often leads to error, and is at best but meretricious."

ELBRIDGE COLBY

# Contents

|  | PAGE |
|---|---|
| Preface by the General Editor | ix |
| Author's Preface | xv |

**CHAPTER**

| 1. Geoffrey Chaucer | 1 |
|---|---|
| 2. Piers the Plowman | 23 |
| 3. John Heywood | 45 |
| 4. Marlowe and "The Heavy Wrath of God" | 61 |
| 5. Two Elizabethans | 70 |
|     Thomas Lodge | 72 |
|     Ben Jonson | 84 |
| 6. Shakespeare and Catholicism | 97 |
| 7. Clerical Characters in Shakespeare | 118 |
| 8. Two Religious Poets | 137 |
|     Robert Southwell | 141 |
|     Richard Crashaw | 152 |
| 9. Three Seventeenth-Century Dramatists | 159 |
|     Shirley and Massinger | 161 |
|     William D'Avenant | 167 |
| 10. John Dryden | 176 |
| Bibliographies | 191 |
| Index | 197 |

# 1

## Geoffrey Chaucer

NEARLY six hundred years ago there walked and breathed and talked upon this earth a man whose name shall never be forgot nor words neglected so long as the English language is spoken and read. True though it be that he wrote in a "lost language," in those first modern moldings of English speech into our own, yet he still has hosts of readers and his fame is wide and justly great. "Dan" Chaucer is and ever will be a landmark in the literature, language, and history of his people. From Dryden to scholars and poets of our modern day, many men in love with the best in letters have wished that his work might be better known to the average man, his simple charm of speech, his direct and intense pictures of life, his clear concept of human character. "It is no longer necessary," says Professor Manly,[1] "to contend that Chaucer is a great poet. His merits have been generally recognized. He is securely placed as one of the three greatest poets who have ever written in English."

Of course he was Catholic. His nation had not in those days strayed from the true Fold, or rather wrenched itself from it. He was not, however, ecclesiastical, clerical, monastic, or Religious by profession or by special interest. He was a man of letters and a man of the world. And so, although

---

[1] John Matthews Manly, *Some New Light on Chaucer* (1926), p. 265. Quotations by permission of Henry Holt and Co., publishers.

we here consider the first great Catholic poet of England, we consider one who centered his literary gifts more upon his country than upon his church. It is perhaps just as well. Otherwise his successors might have burned his books and maligned his gifts and deterred the progress of his reputation. For evidence of the purely religious note and tone in those days of medieval England, there have been preserved for us many a rare gem of verse and many an exalted line of genius. Monk and scribe, here and there layman perhaps or scholar, wrote many a charming poem which reflects the true Faith. Some of these, if you care to see them, have been collected and translated by Mary Segar into an anthology which, in the words of Father Blakely:[2]

> gives us a glimpse into the life of England when England was Catholic, when God was the Father of all, and the deepest mystery of life was the mystery of unfaith. The forebears of some of us . . . needed no flickering rushlight, for faith was the lamp which guided their feet. God, they knew, was our Father, and whatever befell men, was for the best; a simple philosophy at which the world rails, but for which it can offer no satisfactory substitute. . . . With native Catholic instinct, these poets whose names have perished always found the Child with Mary, His Mother, and their tenderest songs are memories of Bethlehem and Nazareth.

It is, as we have said, perhaps just as well.

We shall not remake Chaucer. We shall take him as we find him, a man of letters and of the world, who achieved mastery in his art and permanency in reputation. He had his predecessors, tellers of tales and rhymers of lines. But

[2] *America*, March 3 (1916), Vol. XIV, p. 520.

with him we come to a new high level, where characters live and imagery is vivid, where life is real and idealism is positive and practical. He had his contemporaries, of whom the most distinguished were Gower and "Langland"—but beside him Gower was a mere writer of facile narratives and Langland almost a fanatic. Like his own "clerke" of Oxenford he had many books at his bed's head; yet he was not bookish. In short, the moment we open to a page of Chaucer, we are in the presence of genius, that gift from God which visualizes and vivifies forever the sights which strike the eye and the thoughts which rise in the mind of the outstanding man who indelibly records the men and moods of his time.

I

For more than two hundred years scholars have delved for facts and have created hypotheses concerning the biography of Geoffrey Chaucer. It will be of interest, therefore, to begin by briefly recapitulating their findings.

His birth, now placed about A.D. 1340—possibly a year or so later—is still dated by conjecture. His death is recorded on his tombstone for the year 1400. Students duly scanning successive sheets of legal records and rolls have come upon his name and seem to have established the facts that his father and grandfather were vintners of London, possibly well-to-do wholesale merchants of wine. He appears in 1357 as a page in the retinue of the wife of Prince Lionel, third son of Edward III. He went to the French wars in 1359, and although he saw little fighting, was taken prisoner and had to be ransomed the following year. Recent scholarship—based upon records since destroyed, first reported in 1598 and immediately discredited, but now for new reasons given greater credence—leans toward the belief that he was then educated at the Inns of the Temple for either the law or public life, along with other sons of substantial London men of money. At Christmas of 1368, he was an "esquire" of the king and as such recipient of the gift of a suit of clothes. Until 1378, he was frequently off on the King's Business, on missions abroad, some of them diplomatic, some commercial, and some secret, one of them on another undistinguished military expedition into France, and one (1372) almost a six months' trip to Italy.

For us, this last journey was the most significant, since students have always assumed that it was this trip to Genoa and Florence, in 1372, that furnished him contact with the literary renaissance. The memory of Dante, if not Dante himself, was still fresh and lively. Boccaccio and Petrarch lived. It is probable that he brought manuscripts of these men back to England.

In 1374 Chaucer was appointed Controller of the Customs in London, began to live in Aldgate, and joined—as Professor Lowes has recently remarked—that "distinguished line of public servants who both because of and in spite of their absorption in affairs have memorably enriched English letters. . . . One cannot but recall The Scarlet Letter, which stood in similar relation to the Custom House at Salem, and remember Lamb in India House, and Anthony Trollope writing his novels in his lap in trains and on boats between visits of inspection to post-offices, and Matthew Arnold inspecting schools for a livelihood. . . ." He was off for a time on a trip to Lombardy. In 1385 he became Justice of the Peace for Kent, in days when a justice of the peace was an important, trusted, and responsible officer of the realm. The following year he was elected to Parliament. In 1389, he became Clerk of the Works, to care for, and purchase whatever "stone, timber, brick, shingles, glass, iron, and lead" and see to their use in repairs at Westminster, the Tower, Buckingham Palace, seven royal manors, the royal lodge in the New Forest, and the Mews in Charing Cross, "all with their gardens, ponds, mills, and enclosures."[3] Near the close of his life he became royal sub-forester in Somerset, and returned to lease an "apartment" in London, actually a house, where he died.

Scant though these few biographical facts may be, they have much meaning. It might be possible to imagine Chaucer as a man of letters, brought up in a court reeking with French influence, petted and pampered and preferred, given his daily "pitcher of wine" like a poet laureate (which he was not, of course), and granted remunerative posts in kingly gratitude for the excellence of the manuscript poems which he prepared, had copied, and passed around among the noble "literati" of his time. This it might be possible to assume from the first few biographical facts, but not when the list of home tasks is added to the list of missions abroad. We find that he had actually to work at his appointments at the customs, on the works, and in the forests. Having recently discovered the character of his training at the Temple, we are inclined to assume that he

[3] John Livingston Lowes, *Geoffrey Chaucer* (1934), p. 57. Quotations by permission of Houghton Mifflin Co., publishers.

was also a working, rather than a decorative, member of those foreign missions, in spite of the "suit of clothes" with which his service for the king began. He may have read his books, as he undoubtedly did, but, engaged all his mature life on tasks such as those here mentioned, he also came to know men. The new picture shows Chaucer, in the words of Manly, "not a professional poet rewarded with plums, but a well-trained, hard-working official."[4] He might have read, and read early, the books which were the subject of conversation and allusion among the lords and ladies when he commenced by being a page. More than that, in the world of work, he read human character, and learned the traits of living humans.

In his earliest years, and still under the initial influence of French literature, as well as the current English courtly imitations of the French, he composed numerous short poems—some, like the *Complaint to Pity*, conventionally French in character; some, like the *Complaint of Venus*, free translations; others, like the *Complaint of Mars*, following the French form and precise in metrical skill and elegance of phrase. The *Book of the Duchess*, to mourn the death of the wife of John of Gaunt, and *The Parliament of Birds*, to exalt the marriage of King Richard, were both based upon the French form of a dream-vision, and as Professor Baldwin indicates, though reaching back to Ovid and Cicero, across to Dante and Boccaccio, still began to show a native individual Chaucerian gift,[5] "a larger and more mature originality" and "the close of prentice years."

[4] John Matthews Manly, *op. cit.*, p. 44.
[5] Charles Sears Baldwin, *English Medieval Literature*, p. 200. This and other quotations from this book by permission of Longmans, Green and Co., publishers.

The Italian influence was something new in England. Chaucer brought it in, but remained English. It was a strong stimulus, but did not overshadow his matured powers. The *House of Fame*, the *Legend of Good Women*, and *Troilus and Cressida*—Italian in influence as they were, and the first two keeping the French dream-vision convention—indicated simply narrative facts from the Continent, but they showed skill in dialogue and in characterization which must be innate and cannot be borrowed. The master was ready to write the *Canterbury Tales*.

These titles cannot be exactly dated. One or two are placed by internal evidence. Others are arranged in order by conjecture. We know the outline of his life and of his travels, and something of his acquisition of Italian books. From the facts cited we may reasonably assume that those writings which show French influence were produced early, that those with Italian traces came later. The work which is the finest in technical skill and the richest in understanding of humanity and the world, necessarily came toward the close of his career as an author. It is only thus that we arrange his writings. There were no copyright entries in those days.

II

Yet, one must not imagine that Chaucer was ever a mere copyist, sedulous ape, or imitator. He never fell into the extremes of fantastic metrical form so habitual among French writers of his time. Occasionally he paid some deference to the fictitious "court of love" theories of the Middle Ages common on the Continent, as in the *Franklin's*

*Tale* or the *Knight's Tale*, but he generally transformed and transfigured the commonplaces of the literature of his day. While his contemporary, Gower, was copying, he was utilizing the conventions with the skill of a true artist, making an occasional concession to convention it is true, but still creating new work, and thereby achieving deserved literary immortality. No finer example of his splendid skill among his materials exists, perhaps, than the *Book of the Duchess*. Amid the beauty of a May dawn, it starts with the typical form of a French dream-vision, takes the reader into "green groves thick with trunks of full-leaved trees" (phrases quoted from Frank Ernest Hill's excellent translation), where he meets a sorrowful gentleman. This sad new acquaintance swings promptly into what seems to be a typical lament of the contemporary "court of love" character, still somewhat atypical in that it seems somewhat more finely phrased and infinitely more sincerely versed. It is only in the last lines of the poem that we learn that this is not a surreptitious lover's conventional speech, but the true and perfect lament of a loyal husband who has lost his adorable spouse. The master Chaucer has utilized the forms and traits of a curious contemporary convention to indicate a deep sincerity, sublime affection, and fine idealism.

As if further evidence were needed, grubbing scholars have counted lines, have tallied the words utilized to tell certain tales in Chaucer's "sources" and have compared the total with the number he devoted to the same incidents and topics. They have found that, time and again, he has started to retell an old tale, sometimes compressed, sometimes expanded, sometimes left the original by the wayside entirely, as the drama of the imagined events carried him into the height of truer art. *Troilus and Cressida*, though not by any means a nursery tale, had been recited by countless authors before Chaucer. Now the tale is Chaucer's own. It may bear traces of this antecedent or that, be based upon this history or that piece of fiction. But Chaucer gave its persons real emotions, endowed them indeed with definite character. He did the same in the *Knight's Tale*, took the ancient story of Palamon and Arcite, decked it with the conventions of the courtly love of his age, decorated it with tournaments and pagan temples of Venus and of Mars, and yet made it essentially a deep struggle between love and friendship. "Three quarters of what he wrote had no parallel in the original."[6] By incidents, remarks, and comments, says Professor Dodd,[7] he transformed the conventional story, infused life into what was commonplace to his contemporaries. By so doing he demonstrated his genius. In Baldwin's words,[8] although by our standards of reading he knew but few books and those influenced him much, he contributed to what he copied. Compared with him, the Continental Decameron was mere adroit plot-making, and the work of the nearly contemporaneous Gower in England only easy narration and mechanically smooth verse; neither had Chaucer's climax of character. In the *Franklin's Tale*, also, we have the "court of love" appear again. A faithful loving wife, happily married to a knight, is separated from him by the exigencies of war. A squire who sees her, loves her, but according to the ideas of the time, for two years

[6] Lowes, *op. cit.*, p. 215.
[7] William George Dodd, *Courtly Love in Chaucer and Gower* (1913), p. 117.
[8] Baldwin, *op. cit.*, pp. 191, 197, 199.

keeps silence. Apprized of his hopeless, though typically conventional adoration, she betrays a dangerous pity. She imposes upon him a seemingly impossible task for his seemingly impossible love ("wel I woot my service is in vayn"), which he by sorcery accomplishes. The crisis of the tale has come. Amid the confusion of complicated promises and contradictory loyalties, the plot is resolved to the honor of all, and—if you please—with a moral implication against hasty promises, and errant words. Of this tale, Professor Dodd has remarked: "Gower took fixed ideas of love and left them unchanged. In Chaucer the old conventions become the poet's own. The language he uses to give expression to the passion of love is clever, forceful, and inevitable. His characters live before us as real people. In his maturity, he shows himself always the poet of genius, under whose magic touch commonplaces are transformed and become alive."[9]

If it has seemed that we have considered too much the problem of the love element in Chaucer, particularly an artificial courtly form of love, which was an art to be practised in those days rather than a passion to be felt, it can only be pleaded that such is necessary in comparing Chaucer with his contemporaries. He lived in a world where writers were concerned with such a love. It had its carnal phases, to be sure, but it was principally an idealization, an exaltation of the elemental; it was not the choice of a mate but a sovereign, with all the paraphernalia that goes with sovereignty, all the obeisances and exaltations. It was something quite different, as Chaucer indicates in

[9] Dodd, *op. cit.*, p. 253. Quotations by permission of Ginn and Co., publishers.

the *Parlement of Foules*, from the ideals of the bourgeoisie and the practices of the villein. It was in Chaucer's world, as well as in his books. It is to his eternal credit that he made it something real, that his husband in the *Franklin's Tale* was neither deceived, despised, complaisant, nor wronged, but the honored consort of an honorable woman. But we nevertheless feel a satisfaction in leaving this topic and proceeding to the great masterpiece by which the name of Chaucer will always and everywhere be well remembered.

III

By writing the *Canterbury Tales* Chaucer became not only a great poet, but a great English poet. Some decades ago, when it was believed that Chaucer's father was an ordinary innkeeper of London, it used to be thought that the youth had studied human nature as it came and went by the humble tavern. Then, when scholars discovered the wide range of his reading, there grew a tendency to think that he had created his characters out of whole cloth, and had pieced them together in artificial construction from the books he had scanned. In recent years, according to a theory most prominently promoted by Professor Manly, under whose leadership investigators have discovered close similarities between the prioress, the man of law, the miller and other characters, and certain identifiable individuals in the real world of Chaucer's time and circle of acquaintances, there has been an inclination to argue that Chaucer was depicting "from the life" people he knew. They see in the Canterbury pilgrims not generalized types, but individuals, "strikingly characteristic of their respective stations and callings in life," but also each of them with "some trait not characteristic of the type." Why, else, these protagonists ask, should the distant home of the Reeve be "on a heath well shaded by green trees" unless Chaucer knew such a Reeve? The point is persistently argued, but many think it extreme. Those who think it extreme are not so close to the trees that they cannot see the wood. They claim the work of "identification" has been greatly overdone, doubt if an artist in verse clings always exactly to his models, and prefer to evaluate the completed task as a combination of artistry and observation.

Let it suffice to say that Chaucer has painted a picture of medieval England. It was an England interested in commerce and in wars, in ecclesiastical piety and in reform of ecclesiastical abuses, in its own merry life and in the literature of the world at large, ancient and contemporaneous. It was the world of Caedmon's *Hymn to Christ* and of the beauty-blind Piers Plowman, moral reformer and preacher, whose story, says Professor Baldwin, with all its pictures, was to stir men's souls:[10]

> A thousand of men then thronged all together
> Weeping and wailing for their wicked deeds,
> Crying upward to Christ and to His clean Mother
> To have grace to seek for Saint Truth.
>
> God grant so they may!

It was the world of Chaucer's Parson, who would not leave his poor parish; of Chaucer's Prioress who, for all her worldly daintiness of manner, could tell a marvelous

---

[10] Baldwin, *op. cit.*, p. 185.

# Geoffrey Chaucer

saintly tale of martyrdom; of the Nun's Priest ("a sad-faced pedant with an hundred tragedies in his cell") who could narrate a short-story comedy, replete with conversation and swift in its action. It was a world when religion was infinitely discussed, and religious personages (regular and secular) thronged the towns. Ovid and Boccaccio were not the only books read, nor Jean de Meun and Guillaume de Lorris. In days when every manuscript had to be copied out by hand, there were enough copies of the Vulgate made in the thirteenth century for 5,000 of them still to be in existence. It was a world, perhaps, when physicians like Chaucer's were full intent upon astrology and alchemy "but littel on the bible," and also a world where a courtier and a public officer like Chaucer could be accurately and directly familiar with the Vulgate, with Augustine, with Jerome, and Ambrose, and Jovinian, and we need not say how many more. It was the age of Wiclif and his Poor Priests who sermonized up and down the land. In the chaotic condition of church affairs, there were friars and pardoners, foreign visitors in search of doles, running at cross purposes with local clerics. Any writer representing an age of this sort must be questioned as to religion; but this is no reason to call Chaucer, or John of Gaunt, or Wiclif, for that matter, an "early Protestant." Professor Maxfield in the publications of the Modern Language Association is worth quoting on this phase of Chaucer:[11]

> His attitude toward reform during the period when he was writing the *Canterbury Tales* is fairly clear. He has given us

[11] Ezra Kempton Maxfield, "Chaucer and Religious Reform" in *Publications of the Modern Language Association of America* (1924), Vol. XXXIX, p. 74.

portraits of a few noble Christians and of some who are not true to the Christian precept. The Knight is militant and the Parson is saintly. One extends the faith by righteous arms and the other works for the salvation of men's souls. There was a monk who had done better to have been head of a family. The Friar is too clever, and the Pardoner is a pious fraud. Both rob the secular priests of their religious offices. The Monk, the Friar, the Summoner, all show the defects of the present regime. Sincerity and rottenness stand side by side. How can we interpret Chaucer farther than this?

Chaucer was not only a great English poet. He was the first great English poet. The inherited literature of his time, the imported ideas from countries across the Channel, were inserted into his masterpiece to make an enduring monument, a primary milestone along the road of letters of his nation. In the *Canterbury Tales*, he assembled interesting narratives, told by interesting Englishmen, who are made so vivid in the Prologue and so real in the introductions that they have ever since been taken to represent the England of his time. There is about his art that sympathetic observation and understanding of human nature which makes great writing dramatic. There was also in him, what had scarcely existed as yet in the world, at least in familiar form and true depiction, what William Hazlitt called the "fixed essence of character." Comparing him with his great successor, Hazlitt said:[12]

> The interest in Chaucer is . . . like the course of a river, strong, and full, and increasing. In Shakespeare, on the contrary, it is like the sea, agitated this way and that, and loud

[12] William Hazlitt, *Lectures on the English Poets*.

lashed by furious storms. . . . The characteristic of Chaucer is intensity.

In modern times, we like to watch characters develop. We like to see what happens to people in the face of events, to their hearts and minds. We observe the impact of incidents upon Juliet, of complications upon Hamlet, of circumstance upon Tess of the D'Ubervilles, of conflict upon Stephen Crane's recruit in *The Red Badge of Courage*, of confusion and revolution upon Sidney Carton. Before Chaucer, literature had scarcely as yet achieved characterization. Chaucer's great contribution to literature was to make persons so intense that we considered them as individuals. His characters did not change, as more modern characters do. They had their vices or their virtues. Most of his characters were fixed and their reactions predictable. Only in the *Physician's Tale* and in the *Knight's Tale* is there any inkling of a suggestion that moods might develop into motives. And thus we have him, interesting to read—for the original is not so difficult and the translations of Percy MacKaye, Frank Ernest Hill, and J. U. Nicolson are readable—and rich in knowledge of men and of incidents. Actually ribald perhaps in spots—for as Professor Lowes says, some of his tales, like *Troilus* and the *Miller's Tale*, "with their occasional frank unseemliness, are not milk for babies"[13]—but in other spots virtuous and exalting, Chaucer is illuminating reading.

Obviously in a Catholic estimate of Chaucer's poetry it would be unfair to the reader not to insist that we must sincerely regret—as in his later days Dan Chaucer himself

[13] Lowes, *op. cit.*, p. 217.

did—the indecency of much that he has written. Not unjustly, has it been observed that Chaucer's Retractation, found at the end of some of the manuscript copies of his *Canterbury Tales* and constituting the source of endless comment by bewildered critics, is in reality the most Catholic thing that he has done. He there begs God's pardon for all that he has written amiss.

## IV

Some years ago Professor Frederick Tupper advanced the idea, and not without considerable soundness, that Chaucer, who has for so long been considered merely the teller of tales, was actually preaching. We all have known for many years that the "moral Gower" was deliberately attempting to point his morals to every narrative and to demonstrate the dangers of the Seven Deadly Sins. These, in the Middle Ages, were fixed and well conventionalized: Pride, Envy, Wrath, Sloth, Avarice, Gluttony, and Lechery. Professor Tupper pointed out the medieval tradition of using stories to teach propriety. There is even a stock name for the type: the *exemplum* in literature, originating perhaps out of early moral philosophy. The Seven Deadly Sins were propounded in the *Parson's Tale,* at the conclusion, "to knitte up al this feeste and make an ende." In the general prologue the plan is not mentioned. It may have occurred to Chaucer late, when the course of his writing was already well started. But it seemed perhaps to have come to him. In the prologue to his tale, the Pardoner says: "Then tell I hem ensamples many oon." Aside from the obvious intention apparent in some of the tales, the fact of such a design, according to Professor Tupper, is made especially apparent when we find Chaucer using four plots from the "moral Gower" which Gower used to illustrate four sins.

It were perhaps best to let Professor Tupper continue, quoting from his paper prepared for the Modern Language Association:[14]

> Everyone recalls Chaucer's formal presentation of the Deadly Seven in the *Parson's Tale,* in due accord with the traditional demands of penitential sermons. Even a superficial reader cannot fail to remark his casual references to each and all the Vices in the Canterbury stories.... I have recently discovered that *The Canterbury Tales* offer us yet another treatment of the Sins, not casual but organic.... When in accord with the Ellesmere tradition, I placed the Physician's and Pardoner's stories directly after that of the Franklin, I was struck by a peculiar circumstance.... Here were four of the Seven Deadly Sins, Lechery, Avarice, Gluttony, Sloth. Had this fourfold treatment (I am not insisting now upon the sequence) of the *motif* any significance? Possibly none, unless it appeared that Chaucer had treated the three other sins as well. And then I remembered that he had handled Gower's theme of Pride (inobedience) in the Wife of Bath's Tale, Gower's theme of Wrath (chiding) in the Manciple's, and Gower's theme of Envy in the Man of Law's. Here were the other three, Pride, Wrath, Envy. The entire adequacy of the stories as *exempla* of the Sins was thus established beyond question by Gower's use in four cases, and in the others by their intrinsic fitness for that purpose, and by the

[14] Frederick Tupper, "Chaucer and the Seven Deadly Sins," in *Publications of the Modern Language Association of America* (1914), Vol. XXIX, pp. 96 ff.

testimony of analogues. But did Chaucer, like Gower and the *exemplum* writers, intend that these narratives should illustrate the Vices, or did he ignore utterly the very obvious applications? Then I turned to the Tales themselves, and was confronted by the twofold evidence that the poet deemed them *exempla* of the Sins.

First, each of the stories was accompanied by a preachment against the Sin in question. . . .

But Chaucer went even farther than this in his use of the Deadly Seven as a framework in these narratives. With delightfully suggestive irony, he opposed practice to precept, rule of life to dogma, by making several of the story tellers incarnate the very sins that they explicitly condemn.

This may even be done to the extent that their tales can in no way be regarded as commendable reading from a Catholic point of view. The professor would list:

PRIDE: *Wife of Bath's Tale.*
ENVY: *Man of Law's Tale.*
WRATH: *Manciple's Tale* or *Summoner's Tale.*
SLOTH: Second Nun's Prologue on sloth as contrasted with the "busy bee" St. Cecilia in the tale.
LECHERY: *Physician's Tale.*
AVARICE: *Pardoner's Tale.*
GLUTTONY: *Pardoner's Tale.*

The professor warns against taking the design too literally. He does not believe there is justification for saying that this was Chaucer's whole design. He thinks Chaucer merely illustrated these vices and summed them up in the *Parson's Tale,* using the Deadly Seven as a motif which would be familiar to his readers and to his times. He is cautious, eager not to be too positive in interpreting the fruits of his scholarship. He is gracious and honest enough to say now, twenty years later, that his theory "has not met general acceptance." There is no call here for discussing any controversy on this subject. Suffice it to express the writer's sincere conviction that Professor Tupper's interpretation has contributed not a little to a Catholic understanding of Chaucer. This is important, since Chaucer, after all, must necessarily be considered as a Catholic poet, whatever his shortcomings were in this respect.

As an instance of Chaucer at his best we need only mention the *Physician's Tale*, a marvelous little tragedy of maidenly virtue, chaste in spirit as in mind, patterned after the Blessed Virgin "the pattern of life, showing as an example, the clear rules of virtue." It is a part of the evidence that Chaucer in his noblest work was truly and sincerely a great Catholic poet, as well as a great English poet.

### v

As such we might be content to leave him, at least thus to emphasize him. Yet, we shall not thus abruptly drop him. It were a pity indeed for any Catholic writer to speak of this great master without fuller comment and more complete representation of those perfectly molded gems of Catholic literature which the world at large knows of as the *Prioress's Tale* and the *Physician's Tale*. In the former, a small and saintly lad walks the Jewish quarter of a town, singing always to himself the words of a hymn learned at church: *Alma Redemptoris Mater*. Amidst peril and envy he steps, until vicious wrath and fatal hate strike him low, but even from the depths of the dark well into which he is thrown, there still continues to issue from his pure and holy lips, by some divine miracle, the refrain of that plaintive, hopeful song. Marvelous in its touch, delicate in its feeling, rich in its emotion, dark in its moods, yet intensified with the divine light of perfect faith in a simple child, it is a monument to purity, a masterpiece of art, a classic of Christianity.

Even more tense, emotional, and indeed even more tragic is the *Physician's Tale*, a brief thing, but perfection and power in a little space. It deals with the duties of parents and with the holy virtue of virginity. The daughter of the honorable knight Virginius, beautiful beyond exact description, painted by that skill of Nature alone which gives the rose its matchless red and makes the lovely lily white, is a thousandfold more virtuous even than she is beautiful. Simplicity was her manner. Virtuous, gentle, modest, busy at her tasks, and loath to mix with folly or with frolic. Upon her gazed with covetous eye, a wicked magistrate. He urged a churl to claim her as a daughter, brought the case to court, pretended to believe the lying testimony, declared her father must give her up—and the wicked justice all the while had planned this coup to take and have her for his own. Bereft at law when injustice ruled instead of right, the knightly father considered what he must do, saw no choice but shame or death. The saintly daughter chose her death, and had it by the sword of her own parent. A thousand folk arose in wrath against the wicked judge,

> And caste him in a prison right anon,
> Wher-as he slow him-self.

## Geoffrey Chaucer

The martyred maiden was frankly drawn in character on the model of the Virgin Mary. The phrases Chaucer uses (as Professor Tupper long ago indicated)[15] came from an ancient book of Ambrose of Milan, reflect back to Jerome and Augustine, where vestals of the temples are described as ready rather to die than suffer violation, even though it was said that what was done against their will was no sin in them. Comparable to these was Chaucer's model virgin. After her full consideration of the problem:

> She ryseth up, and to hir fader sayde,
> "Blessed be God, that I shal dye a mayde.
> Yif me my deeth, er that I have a shame;
> Doth with your child your wil, a Goddes name!

A tragedy in the fullest medieval sense, when "tradgeydie is to seyn," it has an exaltation and a direct lesson that is almost beyond description. Others searching through Chaucer may concentrate their attention upon and emphasize the traits of medieval courtly love, with which "faces were disfigured by the malady and woe of love" in accordance with trick traditions, and men were made wan and deathly pale. Others may applaud his skill in recounting the great persons, men or women, of ages past, or delight that he sees the very fields of England "not yet wounded by the plough." Let them find what elaborate pleasure they please in the "complete and realistic picture" of his age, in "the astounding variety of his genius." Let them point to the perfection of imagery in his lines:

[15] Frederick Tupper, "Chaucer's Bed's Head," in *Modern Language Notes* (1915), Vol. XXX, p. 7.

> Her throat, as I have memory,
> Seemed a round tower of ivory.
>
> That first found out the art of song
> Hearing the hammers beating strong.[16]

Such may for merely bookish men amply suffice. For one who has listened with affection to the drumming chords of faith, those Catholic tales strike the deeper, richer note. This is not to say that the *Pardoner's Tale* is not a clever short story, or the *Nun's Priest's Tale* a delightful little moral fable, nor to say that the more ribald narratives have not attractive touches and traces of superior skill. It is merely to say, and to emphasize here, that the Catholic reader will in some of the stories told by old Dan Chaucer, after he had read many books, traveled many lands, known many men of many classes, be able to find not only the things which amuse, entertain, and instruct, but also the things which exalt the soul and strengthen the faith.

[16] From "The Book of the Duchess," as translated by Frank Ernest Hill, in *Chaucer's Canterbury Tales* (1933), pp. 171, 173. Reprinted by permission of Longmans, Green and Co., publishers.

# 2

## Piers the Plowman

"Men will call a universal satirist like Langland a 'morning star of the Reformation,' or some such rubbish; whereas the Reformation was not larger, but much smaller than Langland. It was simply the victory of one class of his foes, the greedy merchants, over another class of his foes, the lazy abbots."—*G. K. Chesterton.*

### I

FACTS regarding the author of *The Vision of William Concerning Piers the Plowman* are practically nonexistent.[1] Between Skeat on the one hand and Jusserand on the other, there have been built up certain assumptions to the effect that his name was William Langland, born about 1331; that he was educated by Benedictines at Malvern near Worcester, took minor orders, never advanced in the Church, and eked out the remainder of his life from 1362 onwards in London, writing, re-writing, revising, and supplementing his original manuscript. First, in four cantos (or *passus*), we have the vision in the Malvern hills of Lady Meed or Bribery, and the woe which she creates in the world amid all classes and conditions of men. Second, we have in cantos

[1] See the summary by John Matthews Manly in *Cambridge History of English Literature*, Vol. II, pp. 1–40.

five to eight, the vision of the Plowman himself, a search for Saint Truth amidst all the evils of this world, its wastes and its deadly sins. Third, we have four cantos, considered by Professor Manly to be probably by another hand, which are more philosophical and less allegorical in the quest for Do-well, Do-better, and Do-best. These three, be it said, signify respectively the active life, the charitable life, and the beneficent clerical life.[2]

We are here, then, upon clearly Catholic ground, probably much more surely so than when dealing with a man of the world like Chaucer of the same period. It was a Catholic world. The Church and the priests who were officers in the Church were common in every place and parish. The monasteries were the repositories of learning as well as of manuscripts. The clergy were the *literati* as well as the readers of the age. The conventional picture of a monk sitting by a window, either conning an old manuscript or transcribing its contents onto a new and richly illuminated parchment of his own—this picture is, like most conventional things, true. However, the desire for reading material did not stop at merely copying what had been handed down from of old time. We have Thomas Aquinas making and reciting very good limericks in his hours of recreation; we have lyric poems of a religious nature which these men penned to the praise of Christ and Mary; we have biographical narrative of the holy men who had preceded them, written down to enlighten future generations and to excite an emulation in the breasts of men to come;[3] and finally we have, as every student of the drama

[2] *Ibid.*, pp. 20, 24.
[3] See G. H. Gerould, *Saint's Legends* (Boston: Houghton Mifflin Company, 1916), which received approval and condemnation, respectively, from reviewers in *The Catholic World* and in *America*.

knows, Christmas, Easter, and "Boy Bishop" celebrations which served distinctly literary purposes as well as devotional and useful ones. St. Francis of Assisi, himself, is supposed to have devised the first Nativity play. In course of time, however, raw humor began to predominate, multiplying such incidents as Noah and his wife boxing each others ears. The assistance of roadside jugglers and performers was secured, beginning thus to make the primary purpose one of amusement, until at length the drama left the cloister, the church, and the churchyard and fell into the hands of professional strolling actors and the trade guilds of the town. But before that period arrived, the moralities and miracle plays had made their presentations primarily ecclesiastical.

While the productions we have here mentioned might have been prepared largely for amusement, there was clerical writing of a more formal nature. Here and there, monk and scribe wrote many a charming song which reflects the true Faith. Caedmon may have sung his pious songs; but Layamon wrote his serious books. Says Layamon at the beginning of his work:

> There was a priest of yore,
> Layamon the name he bore; . . .
> There he read books, verily,
> And the thought upon him fell,
> In his mind he pondered well,
> How folks might by him be told
> Of the noble deeds of old.

Let us avoid the petty quarrels of scholarship in its attempt to argue out details of the assumed life of William

Langland. Mentioning only the generally accepted facts of his clerical training and his undoubted penchant for authorship, we find in his long poem itself the attitude of a serious ecclesiastic. Sincere in his convictions, he adopted the French dream-vision type of allegory to place the truths of his faith against the facts of the tumultuous world as he viewed it. One does not have to be a radical, a John Ball agitator, or a demagogue so to stand. Except that he was not a parish priest and labored with his pen rather than with his perambulating personality, we might well liken him to Dan Chaucer's *Parson:*

> A good man was ther of religioun,
> And was a povre persoun of a toun:
> But riche he was of holy thoght and werk.
> He was also a lerned man, a clerk,
> That Cristes gospel trewely wolde preche;
> His parisshens devoutly wolde he teche.
> Benigne he was, and wonder diligent,
> And in adversitee ful pacient:
> And swich he was y-preved ofte sythes.
> Ful looth were him to cursen for his tythes,
> But rather wolde he yeven out of doute,
> Un-to his povre parisshens aboute,
> Of his offring, and eek of his substaunce.
> He coude in litel thing han suffisaunce.
> Wyd was his parisshe, and houses fer a-sonder,
> For he ne lafte nat for reyn ne thonder,
> In siknes and in meschief to visyte
> The ferreste in his parisshe, muche and lyte,
> Up-on his feet, and in his hand a staf.
> This noble ensample to his sheep he yaf,

> That first he wroghte and afterward he taughte.
> Out of gospel he tho wordes caughte:
> And this figure he added eek there-to,
> That if gold ruste, what shal iren do? . . .
>
> And though he holy were, and vertuous,
> He was to sinful man nat despitous,
> Ne of his speche daungerous ne digne,
> But in his teching discreet and benigne
> To drawen folk to heven, by fairnesse,
> By good ensample, was his bisinesse:
> But it were any persone obstinat,
> What-so he were of heigh or lowe estat,
> Him wolde he snibben sharply for the nones.
> A bettre preest, I trowe that nowher noon is.
> He wayted after no pompe and reverence,
> Ne maked him a spyced conscience,
> But Cristes lore, and his apostles twelve,
> He taughte, but first he folwed it himselve.

## II

Immediately we approach the text itself we are confronted with the manner in which we shall study it. Let us in the beginning state that we shall leave it to the students of language *per se* to worry over word forms and signs of syntax. Let us accept in the most generalized form the broad conclusions of previous students that the first version dates from about 1362, the second, enlarged version from about 1377, and the third version from 1393 or 1398. We may further admit that differences in imaginative power and conciseness of narrative and in successive interpretation of the same facts, evident in re-rendering of definite passages, seem to indicate that the three texts may possibly have come from different hands. What, in such a scrutiny as we are making here, are these varieties and niceties of judgment? It is always possible, as Carlyle said, to agree quite tolerably except in opinion. We have the text and know its approximate dates, and something of the probable general character of its authorship. That will suffice.

Since literature must to a large extent be a reflection of history and life, shall we then go through the thousands of successive lines and explain the political allusions. There is first the famous tale of the mice who would hang a bell about the dangerous cat (B. Prol. 146 ff.), where the mice are the commons, the rats the lords and the cat the king, relating to the good Parliament of 1376, "And leten here laboure lost, and alle her lange studye." When reference is made to the catching of rabbits instead (B. Pro., 133), does it mean Frenchmen? Where the author says, "What this meteles bemeneth, ye men that be merye deuine ye" (B. Pro., 208–9), is he having a laugh at the passive mouse? Yet in the last analysis perhaps the gentle student, like the mice of old, will consider his labor lost and all his long study in attempting such guesswork interpretations.

An attempt might be made to explain away some anachronisms. The passage

For Dauid in his days dubbed knigtes,
And did him swere on here swerde to serue trewthe euere

(B. I., 102–3),

might be checked with the knighting of King Horn with an acolade in another old tale. But it is guesswork again.

## Piers the Plowman

Professor Skeat has cleared up many local allusions. "To Wy and Winchestre I went to the faire" (B., v. 205) refers to old gatherings at Weyhill, near Andover, in Hampshire, and to Winchester fair on St. Giles Hill. Little incidents in Anglo-French diplomacy and warfare account for a long passage (c. iv., 232–243) and a short phrase, "Caleys to selle" (B. iii., 195). Direct political manipulation of the old kings by bribery is reflected in the accusation against Mead, "Yowre fadre she felled, thorw fals biheste" (B. iii., 120). But, though this is less guesswork than the other, it is equally unprofitable.

Another passage leads us to the main issue. In the case of a political pamphlet like Spenser's *Shepherd's Calendar* political interpretation is both useful and allowable. But in a religious poem like *Piers Plowman* the religious element is the useful thing. After an exposition of the Gregorian Rule (C. vi., 147 ff.) and a severe condemnation of those who wandered down the primrose paths, our author says:

And zut shal came a kyng, and confesse zow alle,
And bete you, as the bible telleth, for brekyng of zoure reule,
And amende zow monkes, monials, and chanons
And put zou to zoure penaunce, *ad pristinum statum ire*.

(C. vi., 169–172.)

This has been called an amazing prophecy of the activity of Henry VIII in the abolition of the monasteries, assuming that it would take a powerful man to make the punishment fit the crime. The absurdity is writ large across the face of such a footnote.

First it is laughable to think of Henry VIII having an "object all sublime." The matrimonial and financial advantages of the break with Rome far outweighed any lofty ideal of *ad pristinum statum ire*, and the inflated tone given that revolt has become to all historians except Anglican divines a source of innocent merriment. The passage could not have been a prophecy. The use of the word "confesse" clearly indicates that the "kyng" meant was the one supreme King of Kings to all religions. The tone of the whole poem is distinctly religious, tending toward reform and not revolt. *Omnia restaurare in Christum* (To restore all things in Christ) is merely the modern echo of *ad pristinum statum ire* (To return to the former state). An able scholar, Mr. Rupert Taylor, has said in a volume on *The Political Prophecy in England* that we are too willing to read prophecies into the past. In many a case the man whom glib moderns hail as the "forerunner" of this movement or of that would have run before, not exultingly, but wildly; not with a torch of illumination, but with a red lantern for a danger signal. It all results from looking back rather than throwing ourselves back. We see always through the glasses of our own time, and should not seize with avidity on chance passages, even on sly humor, as tremendously "indicative."

III

Here we come to the crux of the whole matter. We are frankly willing to interpret this long poem from a Catholic writer in a Catholic age as a Catholic poem. Just as Chaucer pictured the same age as seen by a Catholic layman, William Langland pictured it from the viewpoint of a Catholic cleric. His interpretation is less entertaining. It has less sheer narrative interest. Its characterizations are not so clearly individual and dramatic. Its theological teachings are more seriously inserted and more deliberately argued. Its ends are attained by preaching where Chaucer's were by parable. Nonetheless they were teachings and preachings. The reader, or the scholar, who sees in Langland an incipient Martin Luther, and finds in his opinions the groundwork of the religious break with Rome later, is talking—as Chesterton says—rubbish. It is true that there is criticism of clerical practices, but it is also true, as Manly has pointed out, that "... there is nowhere even the least hint of any personal animosity against any class of men as a class, or against any of the established institutions of church or state. The friars have often been supposed to be the special object of attack, but, so far as this vision is concerned, they fare better, on the whole, than do the lawyers. The only notable order of fourteenth-century society that escapes censure altogether is that of the monks."[4]

As any Catholic can testify, our theology teaches that sin or the temptation to sin is not the prerogative of any class. It must be continually guarded against. Every Catholic knows the need of penitence, confession, and absolution. It would have been manifestly improper for a Catholic writer in a Catholic age to go against such a knowledge. He must needs warn all persons against error, in whatever manner, form, or place, it may exist. That is peculiarly his duty, he having professedly made that his department in the general labors of society. As any Catholic can testify also the study of moral theology—and what after all is this allegory of *Piers Plowman* if not a practical study in moral theology?—seems to be mostly a representation of the

[4] *Loc. cit.*, p. 13.

applications of theology to immoral situations. These fundamental factors many students of this poem do not understand. One of the reasons for their misunderstanding also, is a faulty historical label. For decades, until James Harvey Robinson started to set the style in another direction, it was the custom the world over to speak of "The Reformation." Professor Robinson properly labeled it "The Protestant Revolt" and gave the name of "The Reformation" to that movement and cleansing process within the Church itself to eliminate abuses and misunderstandings. In the correct, Robinsonian definition, we have a clear-cut differentiation between a rebel and a reformer. A Martin Luther, a Henry VIII, are rebels. The simplest parish preacher may be a reformer. He is invariably such, in his limited sphere, trying to reform the practices of his parishioners, pointing out to them weekly from the pulpit the errors into which they are falling, pointing out to them the manner in which their errors stand flagrantly forth against the pure backgrounds painted by Saint Truth. Such a preacher was the author of the 3000-line-long poem, whom we believe to have been William Langland. The purely accidental fact that this author has been so unfortunate as to have been introduced to modern readers by men living in England at the time of and therefore somewhat subject to the influence of the bitter controversies aroused by the Oxford Movement and the Newman-Kingsley fracas, is the chief reason for including in this volume the following somewhat close commentaries on misinterpreted passages.

We must therefore disagree with Skeat's religious interpretations time and again and with the annotations of countless other loyal Anglican commentators. Often we need someone to explain the explanation. Too many have been Anglicans believing that an imaginary Renaissance caused an imaginary Reformation, assuming a grandeur unknown to the Protestant Revolt of petty princes, finding attacks where there were none. It is a matter of proper sympathy. The subject of Piers Plowman must be approached with care, with a knowledge of political and social history, a familiarity with the Church and with literature, and with the understanding that this is a difficult problem. Our writer has been studied almost exclusively by Anglican divines, and they have, naturally, misunderstood his simple priest's meaning. Against the background of Chaucer, the teller of tales, and Wiclif, the rampant reformer, they have made two great mistakes. With Wiclif they have mistaken anti-clericalism—exactly what it says, "against clericalism," not "against clerics"—for a Protestant movement, instead of realizing it as a Catholic mood. With Langland they have assumed that he was a critic of institutions when he was merely a critic of men, a plain parson telling sinners to mend their ways. Sometimes in detailed "notes," sometimes in general interpretation, these commentators have erred.

At the very beginning (B. Pro., 3) fault could be found with Skeat's note on "In habite as an heremite, vnholy of workes," taken "to express the author's opinion of hermits in general," for the "vnholy" is here used for the alliteration, and we know that Langland did not think thus "of hermits in general." The word means merely "lay" as opposed to cleric, and is used as is "lewede" in many other passages.[5] Again, he has translated "All of the cardinales

[5] C. X. 140; B. Pro. 25–29; B. Pro. 72; B. iii., 32; B. iii., 148.

atte courte . . . impugne I *nelle*" in the King's Classics as "I *dare* not" when his own vocabulary says "*wish not.*" It is once more a matter of sympathy. Also, speaking of the telling of *un-wise* tales by pilgrims and palmers, we get a clean bill for Langland as a Catholic author. If it were not clear from the rest of the poem it ought to be clear from his widely recognized irony in a passage where he says they "hadden leue to lye al here lyf after" (B. Pro., 49), that he did not believe—as he fears the pilgrims and palmers were all too eager to believe—that they could gain an indulgence, or leave to lie all their lifetime afterward. It is this nominal and unspiritual attitude against which he is continually inveighing.

Coming at the text thus to explain the religious allusions we find a large field for labor, some of the detail of which may be briefly indicated. Lechery (B. iii., 58) is roundly condemned because one of the Seven Deadly Sins. "Seynt James" (B. Pro., 47; B. v., 57) was the most prominent saint of pilgrims. The intercession of repentance for sorrowing penitents (B. v., 485–516) conforms to Church ritual *confessio* "in worde, thoughte, or dedes." The efficacy and the abuse of Sanctuary must be understood for a proper reading of another passage:

> Tyl pardoneres haued pite, and pulled hym in-to house.
> (B. ii., 219.)[6]

A phrase "that in churche wepeth" (B. i., 178) does not refer to an unruly child at service as some might suppose, but to deep and true contrition, as explained, for instance,

[6] Cf., G. M. Trevelyan, *England in the Age of Wiclif*, pp. 115, 138–140.

in Chaucer's *Parson's Tale*. A knowledge of the activities of the Franciscan lay preachers and of the quarrel between the parish priest and the wandering ones explains very easily why we should find a "confessoure coped as a frere" (B. iii., 35).[7]

But such scattered annotations, however valuable in this individual instance, give one only a scattered and a fleeting impression of connection between a manuscript and its time. It is in a wider way that the most valuable interpretation can be done.

## IV

In a broader sense, then, Langland is persistent and insistent in his constantly recurring attention and emphasis on the supernatural in the Catholic faith. It is bad when (C. i., 102) prelates suffer "lewde men in mysby lyve, leuen and deien"; like a good Catholic he finds fault with actual worship of images (C. i., 118–124); and complains that "Here messe and here matynes, and many of here oures arn don indeuoutlych" (B. Pro., 97–8).

Further he emphasizes specific reward and punishments and is ecclesiastical at every turn of a phrase. There is a regular sermon on the Ten Commandments and they are continually mentioned.[8] Men who have "chastite with-out charite, worth cheyned in helle" (B. i., 186), giving us the true sense of charity as love of oneself and one's neighbor in God. Hell is not a mild earthly sorrow or regret, as the French rationalist Holbach would later have us believe, but something real and actual.

[7] Cf. also B. ii., 210; B. ii., 230, and G. M. Trevelyan: *op. cit.*, pp. 89, 92.
[8] C. viii., 204 ff.; B. ii., 78–82; B. vii., 183.

> They shall have and hold, and their heirs ever after,
> A dwelling with the devil, and be damned forever,
> With th' appurtenances of purgatory, in the pain of hell;
> Yielding for this thing, at one year's end,
> Their souls unto Satan, to suffer like pains
> With the wicked in woe, while God is in heaven.
>
> (B. ii., 101–106.)

There we have it: supernatural punishment. Ordinary social reformers are too inclined to dwell on ordinary natural punishment (as the French philosophers, Holbach and Helvetius). At times it seems that Langland is a trifle too inclined to adopt this point of view; but then he flashes through clear and sharp with an insistence on the necessity for true contrition, the loss of heaven and the pains of hell. That is usually his last shot, calculated perhaps to be the most effective.

To avoid this punishment Langland offers the alternative offered by Catholic doctrine. Ruled by conscience, a man may avoid sin (B. iii., 119), but if he has sinned he may properly do penance on earth in place of feeling the pains of hell.[9] But it must be done properly.[10] The whole lesson of the end of Passus II in the B-text is on the harm of improper contrition. What Chaucer wrote out formally in *The Parson's Tale* is here delivered in allegorical form: the divine element in absolution and confession, the essence of true contrition, the resolution to sin no more, the intention to amend one's life by the aid of Divine grace and the help of God, and restitution and reparation.[11]

---

[9] C. iv., 101.
[10] B. iii., 69–72; B. vii., 176; B. xiv., 384–9.
[11] B. iv., 104, 109, 142; B. v., 133, 309, 570, 626; B. v., 276–9, 298–303.

## Piers the Plowman

Langland's preaching applies to all classes, "the lasse and the more" (B. ii., 45), and reminds one forcefully of a scene in a modern novel. In Benson's *The Dawn of All* a Pope is seen for one brief instant, at confession to his attendant priest; and the same theme is developed in two places in *Piers Plowman* (B. v., 607–9; B. vii., 176–8). Just so King Alla in Chaucer's *Man of Lawes Tale* goes to Rome

> ... to receyven his penance
> And putte him in the popes ordinance
> In heigh and low, and Jesu Crist bisoghte
> Foryeve his wikked werkes that he wroghte

The forgiveness of sins and the value of the sacrament of penance as opposed to the Calvinistic theory of predestination is one of the most distinct points of difference between the rebels and the regulars at the time of the Protestant Revolt. This clear statement of the definite claims of the Church came just at the right time—before the vagueness of reactionary Protestant mysticism:

> For it is an unresonable religion that hath rizte nouzte of certeyne. (B. vi., 153.)
> For is no gult here so grete that hys goodnesse nys more. (B. v., 455.)
> Beleve-so or thow beest nouzte y-saved. (B. v., 598.)

And so he writes the book for religious purposes, for

> Hit by-cometh for clerkus Crist for to seruen. (C. vi., 62.)

And he tries to preach, not only in the fields in the day, but to the world when he writes in his study at night

All tymes of my tyme to profit shal turne. (C. vi., 101.)

Thus we find the poem shot through and through not only with chance allusions, but with doctrinaire intent. It was, as we know, supposed to have been written by a secular priest. We are told that it is an allegory. It differs from the allegory of the *Roman de la Rose*, which preceded it, and the allegory of the *Pilgrim's Progress*, which followed it, by the fact that it is distinctly Catholic doctrine. It was an individual morality which the *Roman* put forth with nothing of the supernatural. It was a Protestant morality founded on a reading of the Bible alone which Bunyan produced. This is medieval Christianity; not the glamour of idealized knighthood, as in the Arthurian tales, but the plain and sometimes disjointed preaching of a plain priest.

The most noteworthy resemblances of a superficial nature are that of a pilgrimage on the road, meeting various significantly named characters (B. v., 568 ff.), to *Pilgrim's Progress*, and that of the first setting of the scene that May morning on Malvern hills (B. Pro., 11-19) to the actual stage setting for a contemporary play, *The Castel of Perseuerance*.[12] This, it seems to me, is a very important point. Langland's writing is not very philosophical or argumentative, at least when he talks about actual conditions; his figures are visualizations, pictorial, dramatic, in much the same manner as Bunyan's *Pilgrim's Progress*. The

---

[12] Cf., V. Albright, *The Shakespearean Stage*, pp. 13-14.

essentially dramatic instinct in the human race is seen in the Church services and in other methods of appeal that teach truths which are to be apprehended by persons not versed in the clarity of Aquinas and scholastic reasoning. The drama itself was at the first a method of illustrating and teaching religious truths. All allegories are dramatizations of ideas: and so is *Piers Plowman!*

We might criticize the poem because it is sometimes too digressive, too much inclined to wander at the least suggestion; and the reason is that it is really a didactic piece of work, really a sermon. It is not a consecutive drama, though it uses pictorial representation. It is a sermon in which obvious facts are taken as texts, commented upon and illustrated, as so many of the *Gesta Romanorum* were used. *Infans et Mundus* was dramatic without being a drama. So was *Piers Plowman!*

But before we examine a little further the definite social teaching, apart from the religious emphasis, it must be distinctly understood that this is a book of reform and not of revolution. Where Wiclif took sides and criticized from the outside, Langland produced internal criticism. He thought that each man should do his own task and do it well. "The poor have a poet in Langland." He depicts greed, oppression, knavery and bad relations between the classes. He is not against reform; he is on fire for it; but it must be reform from the irregular, the false, the officious. He has a catholicity in his clear spirit. He would reform the revolutionary reformers as well as the corrupted conservatives.

V

First he preaches vigorously against indifference and ignorance, indifference about religious duties, ignorance of religious faith, ignorance about doctrine, ignorance about the welfare of other folk. Just as a tragedy in dramatic technique is the result of a broken law, lawlessness in life results in like tragic circumstances, and layman and cleric are criticized equally.[13] For sometimes it is, as Carlyle said, "We demanded arrestment of the knaves and dastards, and begin by arresting our own poor selves out of that poor fraternity."

He complains that the peace is violated and enumerates all the wrongs that have been done in the land, including the oppression of the lower classes and the yeomen (B. iv., 48 ff.). He enumerates the various social wrongs in the land.[14] Where the tales of Chaucer, the Falstaff legend, the *Tunnying of Eleanor Runnyng*, are class satire: this is satire on wrong without being class satire. It attacks social injustice.

> Some ploughed with the plough; their play was but seldom;
> Some sewing, some earning, with sweat of their brows,
> The gain which the great ones in gluttony waste.
> (B. Pro., 20–22.)

The poem of Piers the Plowman is a very important

---

[13] B. iii., 93, 148; B. v., 13, 15, 232–239, 314 ff., 404–8, 422; B. vii., 136–7; B. xiii., 384–9; C. iv., 121; C. x., 102–4.

[14] B. i., 19; B. Pro., 129–130; B. v., 314 ff.; C. iii., 129; B. iv., 48 ff.

## Piers the Plowman

social document. But it is more. Let us start by assuming that there is something really wrong with the world and that men are actually in some degree unhappy, that some are overworked and underpaid, and others, overpaid and underworked, remain in idleness, "the norice un-to vyces," as Chaucer says. On the one hand, then, we have a man who foments class hatred, stirs up class struggles, persuades men that happiness is to be gained by active bitterness toward his oppressors. On the other hand, we have the true reformer who thinks that material things of themselves do not bring happiness if one is bitter at heart. The first wants a revolution, the second a reform. And in a complex organism like human society changes must be very slow if we really are to gain the great happiness for the greatest number of people.

Langland is a real reformer. He deprecates the arrogance of the peasantry, the awful pride of a "conscious minority" (as radicals call themselves) who think themselves so much better than the rest of the world. The "letter of love" is despised (B. i., 69), yet real sympathy should rule any movement, sympathy and mutual understanding (B. i., 159 ff.). The proud revolt of Lucifer and his fall is but one example of the intolerant rebel (C. vi., 188–9). The peasants' uprising of 1381 is a case in point—to the conditions of which Langland probably referred directly.[16] He took no sides, he made no distinction between high and low, but only between right and wrong (B. ii., 45). He wished to avoid class struggles, because he knew that neither side was wholly right and neither wholly wrong. He wished to abolish all unkindness (B. i., 190; B. v., 143 ff.), to establish

[16] (B. vii., 62–65.) See also *Vox Clamantis* of Gower as referred to in H. de B. Gibbins, *Industry in England*, p. 161, n. I.

peace, the most precious of virtues (B. i., 150), and to establish love between the two parties (B. i., 157-8.) Both "the lasse and the more" needed improvement, the lower classes needed more material things, the upper more of a spirit of charity and kindness in the ordinary doings of life. And there could be no reform till the world was cleared of bribery, till the king as well as the poor man gained a little idealism, a little of the philosophy of his own and other people's happiness.[16]

So he preaches to kings and knights and tells them to mend their ways, to be mindful of the poor, to restrict the damage of their reckless hunting over peasant fields. Each man should do his duty and gain happiness not through the pursuit of an ambition, but through simple industry. It was no mere chance that when the many people asked Piers the Plowman how they would find truth that he began by simply putting them to work.[17]

All classes must work, without ill feeling or hatred or envy, work with a vigorous sincerity. No loafing would be permitted. No landlord should take advantage of his peasants and no peasants try to gain advantage of their landlord. And from their work well done would come the deserved reward.[18] In this way the world would be bettered. There would be justice and peace in the world, and each man would take his duties and tasks in their proper spirit.[19]

But man would require a guide (B. v., 520). And this

---

[16] B. i., 83-4; B. iv., 134; B. iv., 190-5.
[17] B. i., 94; B. vi., 150, 196-9; C. vi., 147-168; B. i., 173; B. iii., 311-12; B. v., 43; B. v., 147.
[18] B. Pro., 120; B. iii., 307-8; B. v., 24-36, 43; B. vi., 30-3, 67-8, 220; B. vii., 39; C. x., 102-4, 110 ff.
[19] B. iii., 288, 297-302; B. v., 400 ff.

guidance as to the true and proper life he could gain by fulfilling his church obligations, by repenting of his past negligence in word, thought and deed (B. ii., 384–9). So the people and the conditions of the times were, according to Langland, not to be improved by creating ill-feeling, but by direct preaching to the individuals concerned by making each one fully cognizant of what he owed to his fellows. With tremendous power of vivid description and forceful exposition, our author drives home the points of his long sermon. He preaches the Trinity (B. x., 230–248), the perpetual incarnation of God in the Church (B. ii., 29), and explains how the breaking of the Ten Commandments and the falling into the Seven Deadly Sins makes for trouble in this world—trouble for the individual, for the society of which he forms a part, and back again in a circle to the individual. "I am the Truth" has been the proud boast of the Catholic Church. In the days of Langland, as today, it firmly held that it was not a mere vague philosophy apart from life, but an actual rule of conduct which would make the world better. And if the world is worse it is merely because "the ten hestes" are not properly obeyed.

This is the teaching of Langland. He is a preacher preaching a social sermon—emphasizing the Scripture and the Faith in daily life, showing how these can cure the ills of the world if only accepted and followed. His teaching might well be duplicated today in every parish church in the country. It has, in fact, been duplicated to some extent in Leo XIII's famous *Rerum Novarum*. Respecting the rights of all, oppressing none, each man doing his own task, we may work to happiness and content.

Langland taught how it might be done 600 years ago.

And yet today the same sort of class agitator persists in the same sort of class agitation which assails not the evil itself, but the conditions resulting from the evil. If we got rid of the sin of Pride, if we got rid of the sin of Covetousness, if we got rid of the sin of Luxury, if we got rid of all the sins which Langland attacked, and spread abroad a little of the charity and justice and sincerity which Langland advocates, the world today would be a marvelous place. And there would at least be no agitators promulgating hatred. If, like Piers the Plowman, we put all the discontented folks to work, Truth would come to light without a frantic search.

# 3

# John Heywood

I

A QUAINT old English song chants the vacillations of "The Vicar of Bray." Even as mythical as the writer is the character of the Vicar himself. Harrow boys were once taught that the Bray in question was in Ireland, and that the song expressed the difficulties which all Irish clergymen had once to solve. Others reject the Wicklow county parish and fix upon the Berkshire one, but quarrel over attributing the person to the sixteenth or to the seventeenth centuries and disagree even as to whether he died in 1709 or 1565, and as to whether his name was Simon Aleyn, Alleyn, Allen, or Fillon. Whatever the real prototype of this interesting individual—a first study, if you please, of some of "George Birmingham's" interesting individuals—the character remains unique of the Vicar of Bray. Said the elder Disraeli: "He was a Papist under the reign of Henry the Eighth and a Protestant under Edward the Sixth. He was a Papist again under Mary and once more became a Protestant in the reign of Elizabeth. When this scandal to the gown was reproached for his versatility of religious creeds and taxed with being a turncoat and an inconstant changeling, as Fuller expresses it, he replied: 'Not so neither; for if I changed my religion, I am sure

I kept true to my principle, which is to live and die the Vicar of Bray.'"

In such confusing times lived John Heywood.

Bale says that he was born in London, but the usual attribution is to North Mimm's, in Hertfordshire, near St. Albans, in 1497. Pembroke College, Oxford (then named Broadgates Hall), which later fostered old Dr. Johnson, saw him for a while. Chalmers, in his *Biographical Dictionary*, remarks: "But the sprightliness of his disposition not being well adapted to the sedentary life of an academician, he went back to his native place, where, being in the neighborhood of the great Sir Thomas More, he presently contracted an intimacy with that Maecenas of wit and genius, who introduced him to the knowledge and patronage of the Princess Mary. Heywood's ready aptness for jest and repartee, together with the possession of great skill, both in vocal and instrumental music, rendered him a favorite with Henry VIII, who frequently rewarded him very highly."[1]

The life story of any Elizabethan or pre-Elizabethan dramatist is at best an unsatisfactory affair, and John Heywood is no exception to the rule. It has been a favorite task for students, inspired by the writings of these men, to spend many an hour in obscure libraries, where books and manuscripts are covered with the dust of decades and facts obscured by the passing of time, and there, finding pleasure in painstaking research which few persons comprehend and fewer appreciate, to evolve and defend elab-

---

[1] Appleton Morgan, in his article, "Shakespeare—His Third Centennial" (*The Catholic World*, April, 1926, pp. 21, 22), is at some pains to identify poor Yorick, "the king's jester, . . . a fellow of infinite jest, of most excellent fancy," as our own John Heywood.

# John Heywood

orate theses on the literature of the period, to produce careful introductory notes for old plays and to publish scholarly dissertations in the universities of England, Germany, and America. And their work has not been in vain; certain facts are from time to time brought to light which help to round out our portraits or to fill in the spacious and vague backgrounds.

Heywood's work was so scattered, in many respects so piecemeal, retrieved from obscurity by so many delvers here and there, that only recently have we moderns come to appreciate such a many-sided man. With his editing by John S. Farmer, however, and the excellent critique and biography written by Professor Robert W. Bolwell in 1921, the old gentleman takes a clearer position and we have a fuller view. Any reader of the Bolwell book must conclude that Heywood deserves rank as a principal Catholic poet, who died in Catholic exile.

It is not necessary to recite many of the unrelated details of this life of multifarious occupations. We need mention only a few. Heywood left Oxford at the age of seventeen, probably in order to enter the King's service, possibly in the King's choir of the Chapel Royal, as a court singer. Becoming closely acquainted with Sir Thomas More, with William Roper, William Rastell, John Rastell, the Catholic printer whose daughter he married, staunch Catholics all, he moved in brilliant and excellent circles, of high intellectuality.

In 1544, so ardent was his religious belief, he was found guilty of treason, for some months held in prison awaiting sentence, and suddenly pardoned by the King.

From 1521 onwards Heywood is supposed to have

received an annuity of ten marks as player on the virginals; he was in 1522–3 made a "freeman" of London and "admytted into the liberties" of the city; and we know that from 1538–44 he received quarterly the sum of fifty shillings in the same capacity; so it is not exaggerating these records in the *Privy Purse Expenses of the Princess Mary* to say that the precocious youth of that godchild of Cardinal Woolsey, who played so well on the virginals, was due to Heywood's instruction.

In January, 1536–7, and March, 1537–8, he had received money in connection with the famous children of Paul's, who played before the Princess Mary; "his children," the record says. So if More's wit, as lasting keen even as the executioner's ax, delighted Henry, Heywood's pleased Mary. At her coronation in 1553 in St. Paul's Churchyard he "sate in a pageant, under a vine, and made to her an oration in Latin and English."

Chalmers says that he died abroad; others, in London. At any rate, in 1587 he was "dead and gone." And there passed an interesting individual, a loyal Catholic author, whose loyal son resigned a Fellowship at All Souls in 1558, refused to conform to Elizabeth's Church and went to Rome to become a Jesuit.

John Heywood was friend to Sir Thomas More, tutor to Mary Stuart, saved his neck by his wit under Edward VI, was persecuted out of England by "the good Queen Bess," and ended his life at ill-fated Malines, short of funds and stripped of his possessions by Spanish and German soldiers who little realized who was the old man they so roughly handled. His interludes are indeed the most noteworthy elements in the development of the early British

# John Heywood

drama, and his parable of the spider and the fly depicts, with remarkable success, social injustice and religious disturbance in England during the years between the reign of Henry VIII and Elizabeth the imperious.

> Eche man as he vsythe the gods gyfts of grace,
> So schall he have in hevyn hys degre or place.
> But, mark thys chefe grownd, the sum of scrypture saythe
> We must walk with these gyfts in the path of faythe.

Court wit, practised musician, and capable poet, his technical skill and high piety have been overshadowed by the mere fact that some of his apparently minor work happened to mark a distinct step in dramatic progress. Yet, when we read of the position usually assigned him with regard to the English stage by historians of literature, we must not forget the faith and piety of the man who sincerely wrote:

> I desyre no number of many things for store;
> But I desyre the grace of God, and I desyre no more.

## II

The major non-dramatic writings of John Heywood are:

*A Parable of the Spider and the Flie* made by John Heywood. Imprinted at London in Flete Strete by Tho. Povvell. Anno. 1556.

*John Heywoodes workes.* A dialogue conteynyng the number of the effectuall proverbes in the Englishe tounge, compact in a matter concernynge the two maner of maryages. With one hundred of Epigrammes: and three hundred of

Epigrammes upon three hundred proverbes: and a fifth hundred of Epigrams. Whereonto are now newly added a syxt hundred of Epigrams by the sayde John Heywood. Londini. Anno christi, 1562.

The most part of these epigrams is a series of phrase turnings which lend a touch of the truth to Chalmer's mention of Heywood's "ready aptness for wit and repartee," if the anecdote of the Duke of Northumberland's table had not already done so. The clever juxtaposition of words was quite the thing in these days: the Elizabethan songsters were almost upon us and Tottel's *Miscellany* appeared in 1557. His *Description of a Most Noble Lady* is as pretty a compliment to Mary Stuart as ever rhymester paid to lady in sonnet cycle or other verse:

> Amongst her youthful years
>   She triumphs over age;
> And yet she still appears
>   Both witty, grave and sage.
>
> I think nature hath lost her mould
>   Where she her form did take;
> Or else I doubt that nature could
>   So fair a creature make. . . .
>
> It is a world to see
>   How virtue can repair,
> And deck such honesty
>   In her that is so fair.

So he can blithely write of "vanished vanity," ask his

## John Heywood

friends to "keep possessed possession peaceably," and tell how "glory past increaseth present grief." He can chant a quaint and courtly lover's regret in *A Ballad of the Green Willow* ("an old thing it was" which Desdemona sang in slightly altered form, for it would not go from her mind), and he can also praise in a ballad "the most excellent meeting and like marriage between our Sovereign Lord and our Sovereign Lady, the King's and Queen's Highness," when Philip of Spain and Mary Stuart of England were joined together in 1554.

> Some count no charge
> To talk at large;

so Heywood penned a *Ballad Against Slander and Detraction* which deserves not to be forgotten; and the traitorous taking of Scarborough Castle moved him to a "ballet" urging folk "to 'bey their King and Queen."

But though he won some fame for his cleverness in shorter verse and longer drama, one of the most significant facts about Heywood centers around his *Parable of the Spider and the Flie.* He was thoroughly awake to the social and economic shortcomings of the people of England, of high and low of each degree.

It is only necessary to look at the date of *The Spider and the Flie*, 1556, and to read in the "Conclusion" that it was begun twenty years before, the year of the Pilgrimage of Grace, 1536, and then we have some basis for understanding the poem. It is said that a contemporary writer in *Holinshed's Chronicle* remarked that neither its author nor anyone else could "reach into the meaning thereof."

But it is not so difficult. The flies are the Catholics, the spiders the Protestants; Queen Mary is the housemaid who comes in at the last minute (1553) and sweeps aside the arrogant cobwebs, executes the commands of the absent master (Christ) and her mistress (the Church) by killing the oppressive spider. Reading the tale thus, we get the whole story of Robert Aske and the Pilgrimage of Grace, with the patronage of St. Cuthbert and the banner of the five wounds.

It must not be forgotten that the conditions of the Peasant's Revolt of 1381, with its John Ball, "the mad priest of Kent," was reflected in Langland, nor that More's *Utopia* of 1515 likewise showed an insight into social and economic affairs. It must not be forgotten also that the enclosure of common lands by the lords, and even of peasant "strips," made the Pilgrimage of Grace as much the result of economic as of religious affairs, and probably even more.[2] The large land owners, who benefited from the enclosing of land, and the new nobility, the houses of Russell, Cavendish, Seymour, Grey, Dudley, Sidney, Cecil, Herbert, Fitzwilliams, and Rich, who benefited financially from the suppression of monasteries, were ranged against the Catholic peasantry—the spiders against the flies.[3]

> The towns go down, the land decays;
> Great men maketh nowadays
> A sheep-cote in the church.

It was not only the appropriation of the monasteries, but

[2] H. de B. Gibbins, *Industry in England*, pp. 215–218.
[3] Goldwin Smith, *The United Kingdom*, Vol. I, pp. 334–336.

their appropriation for sheep, involving all the commercial changes and industrial prosperity to follow.

*The Spider and the Flie* shows how the spider wants to appropriate all the small openings in the window to which the flies had previously had free access—the common lands, of course. The figures, even the number of men actually engaged on each side in the military struggles, are not far from accurate, and the lack of organization among the flies is aptly condemned. "Force without order winneth victory seld." The idea is repeated in *The Foure PP:*

> Men cannot prosper, wilfully led;
> All things decay where is no head.

There is no doubt as to who is meant when Heywood speaks of the spiders as gentlemen who set exorbitant taxes and raised rents against the yeomen flies.[4]

The form of the poem is that of a dialogue with slightly shifting characters—a dialogue which proves a point as clearly and conclusively as ever did any question-and-answer product of scholastic philosophy. This is also the form of the dialogues *Wit and Folly* and *Gentleness and Nobility*.

There is another similarity between this parable and the writings of Langland and More—a pertinent criticism of the lawyers and legal methods. "Reason, law, custom and conscience," we are told, should be the standards of judgment; there is too much "rude railing" in the courts; too much imprisonment without proof; quibbles are displayed

---

[4] The subject of the transmission of feudal dues is also a subject of discussion in Heywood's *Gentleness and Nobility*.

in all their folly of men who "grant" yet do not absolutely grant; there is "meed" in the shape of rewards and bribery; one of the arbiters, "learned in the school of ignorance," quotes Latin, "spoke much and understood little." Justices are shown as Swift showed them later with no concern for absolute right and wrong, but only for the technical agreements or disagreements, "to try how good or ill custom is, is no part of our charge." And, finally, they are told that all should be equal before the law, that credence is a matter to be given not on the basis of rank, but according to evident honesty.

So, on the principle of equality, we return once more to recall the lack of class feeling in Langland and More, when they were commenting on good and evil. The Socialistic rhyming of John Ball is repeated:

> When Adam delved and Eve span,
> Who was then a gentleman?
> *(Gentleness and Nobility.)*

There is "dishonesty in spiders and in flies both"; noblemen should be "keeping themselves in their bounds as they ought" and the ploughman should "desire no more than is needful." Good and bad of all degrees are condemned, as Langland had condemned them. And even when enemies die, Heywood is moved rather to "lament their false facts than rejoice their false falls" (*The Spider and the Flie*).[5] Each must do his own part. We find it thus stated in *The Foure PP:*

---

[5] The same idea is repeated in the "ballet" on the *Traitorous Taking of Scarborough Castle*.

# John Heywood

> What helpeth wyll where is no skyll?
> What helpeth skyll where is no wyll?
> For wyll or skyll, what helpeth it
> Where frowarde knaves be lackynge wyt?

Like the phrase "keep possessed possession peaceably," these lines represent more than a mere playing with words.

These were terrible times in which Heywood lived and of which he wrote, saying that it were better sometimes to be judged by your foe than by your friend, for your foe might attempt to conciliate and be lenient through fear and your friend would probably be treacherous from fear.

> Fear pierceth deep as hunger make ye sure.
> The father his son, and the son his father,
> The wife her husband, and the husband his wife:
> The brother, his brother, all these we gather
> To have seen (compelled by fear), where fear was rife
> Bewray and betray each other in fear of life,
> Sealed see we no natural a foolish kind pelf,
> But he will hang his father to save himself.

The Vicar of Bray alone escaped, and how ever he did is a veritable marvel.

### III

The chief dramatic writings of John Heywood are: *The Pardoner and the Frere* (1533); *The Play called foure PP* (1545, 1533); *A mery play between Johan-Johan the husbande | Tyb his wyfe | & syr Jhan the priest* (1533); *The Play of the Wether* (1533); *The Play of Love* (1533), and *A Dialogue Concerning Witty and Witless* (first printed from original MS. 1846).

The last three of these are scarcely more than academic disputes, little more exciting, so far as dramatic action is concerned, than a modern formal debate. *The Play of Love*, for instance, contains but a single stage direction. Carefully arranged argument with repartee and rebuttal make up the most of these three.

But the other three are more interesting and we begin to realize why Heywood is "important in the history of English drama as the first writer to turn the abstract characters of the morality plays into real persons," and how his interludes "link the morality plays to the modern drama, and were very popular in their day."

The figures which walked across the stage were not the "Manhode," "Folye," or "Perseueranaunce" of the moralities, but actual living persons out of sixteenth-century England; and they carried not the symbolic properties of the early liturgical dramas, but real articles in use at the time by the very persons in the audience. The situation of Johan-Johan in the "mery play" in which he appears is typical of the change: he sits at one side of the stage chafing a candle and mending a pail by the fire, while his wife and Sir Johan eat the whole of a new pie which was to have been shared each-and-each. After touching on the broadest of broad farce, dealing freely with the boldest of social satire and ridicule, they typify the departure of the drama from the church, the churchyard, and even from church auspices and supervision. The theater was becoming secularized. In the process of secularization it took over some of the characteristics of the humbler and more homely tales which delighted the middle ages. Chaucer's *Miller's Tale* and his *Reeve's Tale* are a little coarse in tone, but in character they touch very near the type of these "mery" interludes of John Heywood. It was the true beginning of English comedy.

Still, there was connected with it an element which had scarcely ever been absent from medieval story telling of the French farce and the *fabliaux* type, a pointed emphasis on class satire. Sir Johan is unkindly treated by implication, "giving absolution upon a bed"; the futility of pilgrimage faith without worldly works of worth is spoken of in the palmer (*The Foure PP*); and others are not spared, the sellers of indulgences, as is just, least of all:

> Right seldom is it seen, or never,
> That truth and pardoners dwell together.
> (*The Foure PP*)

The long description of the various "virtues" of the many relics which the pardoner carries with him seem to take us back to Merlin and the world of enchantment, to Minnie, Morgan le Fay, and invisible knights. Or they recall the biting criticisms and fervent condemnations of Langland, who could not abide the pardoners masquerading as priests and placing more confidence in Bishops' seals and Papal letters than in right living and clean thinking.[6] But it is often the case, as we found when looking at Heywood's nondramatic writings, that he criticizes all who need criticism without distinction. This was the mode of Langland and More, and also of Heywood.

[6] Cf., *Piers the Plowman;* Text A., Prol. 68–75.

Professor Pollard has gone so far as to reason thus: "According to a tradition which there is no reason to doubt, he was a friend of Sir Thomas More, while we know that four of his plays were printed by William Rastell. . . . Rastell, at this time, and More, throughout his life, held those views as to church-policy to which we know that Heywood consistently clung. The attitude of firm belief, with an absolute readiness to satirize abuses, which we find in Heywood's plays, was exactly characteristic of More, and it does not seem fanciful to believe that it was partly to the author of the *Utopia*, and to the circle of which he was the center, that Heywood owed his dramatic development."[7]

*The Play of the Wether* is very nearly the most interesting of all. In it we have various persons brought before Jupiter demanding satisfaction of various desires and aversions with relation to the sort of weather which suits them best. The huntsman lord wants it clear without wind; the merchant wants cool breezes for his ventures abroad upon the deep to suit their courses; the woodranger, a lazy rogue, wants extreme storms; the water-miller wants always a steady rain and no wind; the wind-miller no rain and steady winds for his grinding; a gentlewoman wants her beauty protected from both storm and sun; a "launder" (laundress) wants hot sun for her clothes-drying days, and the small boy frost and snow for the joy of youthful sports. These people all speak to Merry Rysert—and quarrel among themselves—and when Jupiter hears the demands

---

[7] "Critical Essay" in Charles Mills Gayley, *Representative English Comedies* (1903), p. 5, quoted by permission of The Macmillan Company, publishers. See also Robert W. Bolwell: *Life and Works of John Heywood* (1921), pp. 95, 105, 109–110.

# John Heywood

he says that each shall have his wishes. He accomplishes the compromise of giving each his own part, in his own district and portion, by ordaining that everything shall be left "even as it was."

In a time of such turmoil, amid religious and economic uprisings, lordly greed and servile rage, intellectual expansion and commercial change, this little *Play of the Wether* comes as a fit lesson for the times. "Even as it was" each could work out his own path for right if only he would not ask and demand too much. It was the lesson of *The Spider and the Flie* as well as of this play. It was the lesson of every true reformer of every time, seeing that pride and covetousness and greed are at the bottom of most social troubles, that if individuals were all reformed there would be no need for revolt nor for the formation of new institutions.

## IV

If the Vicar of Bray is in some sense characteristic of the age in which Heywood wrote and lived, there is another characteristic far more important—the Commercial Revolution which was just about getting under way. In *The Play of the Wether* he has sketched something of the service done by merchantmen through the world, East, West, North, and South, bringing home the wealth of far lands in daily danger of their goods and life. Stressing as we shall in these essays literature as a reflection of social and economic, as well as intellectual history, there is scarcely a better way to end than by quoting another of Heywood's merchants (*Of Gentleness and Nobility*), who speaks in defense of the trade he plied—the trade which was to make the future greatness of Elizabethan England in commerce, as the drama made it great in literature.

> I say the common weal of every land
> In feat of merchandise doth principally stand.
> For if our commodities be uttered for naught
> Into strange land and no riches brought,
> Hither therefore we should come to beggary,
> And all men driven to live in misery.
> Then we noble merchants that in this realm be,
> What a great wealth to this land do we;
> We utter our wares and buy theirs good cheap,
> And bring them hither with great profit,
> And pleasure daily cometh to this region
> To all manner of people that here do won.
> Furthermore, ye see well with your eyes
> That of strange lands the commodities,
> We have such need of them that be there,
> That in no wise we may then forbear,
> As oil, silk, fruits and spices also,
> Gold, silver, iron and other metals more . . .
> And I spend my study and labor continually,
> And cause such things to come hither daily,
> For the comfort of this land and commonwealth.
> And to all the people great profit and health.

# 4

# Marlowe and "The Heavy Wrath of God"

WITHOUT a doubt one of the most stupendous events for any adventurer in literature is a first reading of Christopher Marlowe's play, *Dr. Faustus*. This at least is a masterpiece which deserves to be forgotten so that the same thrill and elevation may come with each new reading. That Elizabethan dramatist had a truly meteoric career. Out of Cambridge he came with others who were called the "University wits," flashed for a moment across the darkness of an undistinguished British stage, and lighting an hour or two was gone. He left his imprint, however, indelible upon the English drama. Thereafter the chronicle history play became a heroic work of art, not a mere chronology. Thereafter the blank verse of his "mighty line" sounded sonorously across the boards for many years to come. Thereafter there was power and strength to theatrical literature: Richard III, whatever royal genealogists may say, is a lineal descendant of Barabas, Faustus, and Tamburlaine. From the cheap social satire and cheaper buffoonery, from the dry chronicle catalogue of political event and the dryer classical forms of Seneca, he led his art in dignity and grace.

> From jigging veins of rhyming mother wits
> Aud such conceits as clownage keeps in pay,

he marched in stately measures which Shakespeare was glad to tread and countless other artists anxious to imitate.

Yet, however great his artistic conquests, the chief value of Marlowe to our modern views of literature and life does not concern any meticulous drawing of analogies or presentation of parallel passages, nor in any discussion of purely literary origins. He stands for something far greater. He stands for Tragedy, complete and everlasting. He is a prime example of a man who has gained the whole world without recking the loss of his own soul.

Back to the Greeks we go. Back to the old Aristotelian definition of tragedy, as the inevitable result of a broken law. In three characters Christopher Marlowe depicted this tragedy of the broken law and the fall of man, no longer the mere fall of princes in the medieval conception of tragedy as the adventures of the unfortunate great. Tamburlaine was ambitious for military power and sought to be a superman. Barabas was ambitious for gold, "infinite riches in a little room." Faustus was intellectually ambitious for power and sold his soul to Satan for the temporary skill of the magician. Each broke a law and met the just punishment he deserved. Each gained a passing physical victory, but met a psychic defeat—which was followed by the inevitable downfall. The spiritual was neglected; the material conquest was achieved; but the spiritual failure came as a final act of retributive justice. Of what avail were the riches of the Jew of Malta, the skill of Tamburlaine "to entertain divine Zenocrate," or Faustus' pleasure in "the face that launched a thousand ships and burnt the topless towers of Illium," when the degradation which these achievements entailed descended upon the offenders against divine and moral law?

Nor is it fantastic to speak thus of Marlowe, as represented in his three greatest plays, for an almost perfect analogy existed between the characters he depicted on the stage and the character of the man himself. Here was a fresh young university student come up from Cambridge. In London he gained the success deserving to his genius and to his idealism. But at the same time he was gaining that success he was compromising the high ideals for which he had been taught to stand.

It is probable that Marlowe was actually under suspicion for a time as being a Catholic, but no positive statement can be made that he ever professed the Faith. In his dramas, as already indicated, the Catholic lesson is driven home that unrepented sin will meet its punishment, "to be plagued in hell."

What we know of his own life is that it contains material for a stupendous tragedy in the Aristotelean sense. We have here the old theme of a broken law and its retribution as called for by poetic justice. In the ways of God, of course, the divine retribution need not take place in this life. Spiritually Marlowe courted disaster by his intimate connection with atheistic associates who paraded their atheism in an organized form before the society of their day. How low he fell materially we cannot say with any certainty. Dr. Hotson in his study on "The Death of Christopher Marlowe" (1925), which he based on documentary evidence in the Public Records Office, rejects the traditional account of the poet's tragic end—stabbed to death with his own dagger amid a swarm of outcast knaves, in a quarrel over a disreputable wench. Instead we are told that he was killed at an inn, after violently attacking his companion in a dispute that arose over payment of the bill. Critics are not all convinced of this account either. But however the sudden end came to him, at the prime of his power, due to some uncontrolled passion as these accounts agree, we have here a broken law and the stage set for a tragedy in the ancient sense. Well might it have been he, and not Faustus, who exclaimed:

>O lente, lente, currite noctis equi!

and well might he have borne in mind the tragic words placed by him on the lips of Faustus:

>Think'st thou that I who saw the face of God,
>And tasted the eternal joys of heaven,
>Am not tormented with ten thousand hells?

This was the greatest tragedy of the Elizabethan age: greater than any play was this actual living tragedy completed by what Faustus would call "the heavy wrath of God," and moderns "the moral consequence."

Yet when we skip blithely over a couple of hundred years or more we find a change in the literary ideals of the English-speaking people. We come to the "period"—delightful phrase dear to the academic mind—called the Age of Romanticism which saw the full fruition in letters and in politics of an independent, individualistic philosophy of life, protesting against authority—that philosophy which rose with, or as a part of, or as a result of the Protestant Revolt. In a steady tendency toward simplification by eliminating formal restraints, men walked down the lane of the least resistance and broke into open rebellion at the end of the eighteenth century. Not only to political action do the words of Madame Roland apply: "Liberty, what crimes are committed in thy name!"

Back to a pure and unregulated nature did the world see itself marching. In literature there was rejection of the old manners and materials in favor of more independent forms and ideas. They vainly called it a greater sincerity and a slighter formality. According to the romantic ideal, each poet was a prophet, priest, and seer who interpreted the things of nature, humanity, and his own feelings in his own way. It was the age of introspective individualism. Wordsworth and Whitman are its apostles; the tragedy of the broken law was forgotten because law had been discarded.

Out of this general tendency grew the sentimental romance which may amuse, but also undoubtedly teaches false ideas. There are thousands of examples which might be adduced from nineteenth-century fiction, but we shall confine ourselves to the career of Marlowe. And first we must understand his thesis—a thesis which he did not put into personal practice. For not Tamburlaine, nor Barabas, nor Faustus represents Marlowe's own intention so well as Paris in Lyly's play, *Contentment Is My Wealth*. The lesson of Marlowe's three leading personages was not acceptable in nineteenth-century England, which continued to protest against rules and dreaded responsibility. His plays were not very well liked. But the treatment which his life itself has received is even more indicative of the modern mind. In 1837 Richard Hengist Horne published a drama dealing with the tragic end of this most promising of Elizabethan songsters, based on the long-accepted tale. But he went to great pains to make Marlowe's passion for the wench a worthy one and to have the girl change her way of life. It was the typical nineteenth-century interpretation, giving an intense story, but one neither true to facts nor plausible. It was the characteristic refusal to see the tragedy which must result from misconduct. It insisted on false external sentiment. It was romance, and therefore not real. Then, as if to prove that we have not as yet discarded these shifting, irresponsible sentiments, we bought and read and praised two more similar, idealized narratives based on the same tragic career. In 1901 Josephine Preston Peabody (Mrs. Lionel Monks) published *Marlowe: A Drama in Five Acts*, in which, though in *The Wolf of Gubbio* she has shown the true Franciscan spirit and a thorough sympathy with the virtue of rigid Catholic principles, this authoress revels in distorted romanticism and makes Marlowe repent of his sins at the last moment of his life. Similarly in 1913 Mr. Alfred Noyes published in *Tales of the Mermaid Tavern* another narrative of the death of Marlowe, in which he likewise adds an unwarranted repentance and spreads over all an unreal glamour of simulated virtuosity.

Now, no one has a right to dispute with these writers for painting the figure of Marlowe strange and strong. But the tendency to condone his actions because he was—in the modern romantic sense—a poet is contradictory to right morality and destroys the virtue of his biography.

## Marlowe and "The Heavy Wrath of God"

The tale is the story of failure, self-inflicted because he sinned in a spiritual and in a material way, by denying his God or at least associating with those who did so in an organized way, while he failed to govern his own turbulent passions. It is the tragedy of the broken law. Yet the moderns dodge the issue and spoil the moral.

This inclination to sentimentalize over genius and to ascribe to it virtue, instead of condemning its vices, is likewise seen in many of our modern romances. Dauville's story of the career of Gringoire and McCarthy's story of Villon in *If I Were King* are examples of the same thing. Ribald taverners with a facility at rhyming as well as murder and gaming are glorified because they defied institutions, because they defied social conventions, because they broke laws whose violation should have involved them in stupendous tragedies. We have, indeed, gone far from the straightforward morality of Aristotle.

This other question of a deathbed repentance is more difficult to handle, but the answer seems fairly clear. The idea of the forgiveness of sins in a definite and exact way is as old as Christianity, and God's goodness is infinite. Our quarrel is not with Marlowe himself, but rather with these moderns who have written him down in such a manner that their fictitious characters of Marlowe could not be convincingly repentant. They end their narratives in a vaguely romantic way and lack the power of a definite tragedy. Their lesson lacks definiteness and strength.

And here we come to our chief point of disagreement with modern literature: the old, old contrast between the classical standard and the romantic irresponsibility. Ever since Wordsworth and Scott our writers have tended to some degree to be individualists, to preach independence and to slight the definite formality of ordinary laws which have been established in Catholic practice, and whose wisdom stands confirmed by long experience with problems of morality. In Wordsworth, in Tennyson, in Browning, in Swinburne, in Tagore, the inclination has been to emphasize individual rather than higher origins for our moral motives. Tricked out in pleasing phrase, ideas of an incomprehensible feeling have been put forth as "deep" and "true." It is pantheism which they teach, and an indefinable and untrustworthy emotional reaction of an unreasonable sort. What the world needs is not a substitution of vague poetic idealism for religion, but a clear consciousness of the difference between the refined and the vulgar, between right and wrong, between black and white. These men of letters condemn exact definitions, and exalt introspection and psychological experience—forgetting that true traditional definitions are the long-standing result of painful mistakes in previous experience. They want to make the mistakes all over again, and fear to look ahead lest they learn that all their experiments may lead them in the end to the same definitions which they now reject.

The threefold temptation of Christ in the wilderness corresponds in some degree to the three plays of Marlowe. Barabas resolved to covet gold, Tamburlaine military and political mastery, and Faustus "a world of profit and delight." Marlowe tried to show the fruitless folly of their choice. And we very much fear that the world of today, if it is to be judged by its expressed opinions—as we have judged it from its mistaken conception of the character of Marlowe—would choose to shout in loud tones: "Freedom from restraint!" and follow in the footsteps of Barabas, Tamburlaine, and Faustus. It would be individualistic, almost individualistic enough to urge that Christ should have yielded to the temptations of Satan for the valuable "experience" that might have resulted therefrom. But the world must heed the lesson to be read in both the works and the life of Marlowe, that there is no way to hide "from the heavy wrath of God," that the Aristotelian idea is still sound, and that there is always one inevitable consequence of a broken law—tragedy.

# 5

## Two Elizabethans
*Lodge and Jonson*

THE AGE of "good Queen Bess," as some of her admirers were wont to call her, is regarded as of tremendous importance in English history and English literature. To the historian it marks the end of the strong Tudor monarchy, to the *litterateur* it means an epoch of lyric sweetness in song and conclusive strength in drama, to the economist a period of commercial expansion unequaled in the history of the world, to the geographer an age when new lands were discovered and new colonies founded, when Hawkins and Raleigh, Drake and Cavendish, privateers and merchant adventurers, were building Britain's greatness across seven oceans, when bread was cast upon the waters which should return after many years with glory everlasting and the lordship of the sea.

It was a time when, in letters and in commerce, men were able to rise quickly to posts of honor. Distinctions between classes never were before, nor have been since, so little regarded as they were then. University wits, masters in arts from Oxford and Cambridge, mingled on the stage and in the taverns with grammar-school lads from Stratford and unschooled drunkards from Cheapside. Then, if ever, was a true democracy of letters. So let it not seem strange that we link together the names of Thomas Lodge, son of the Lord Mayor of London, and Ben Jonson, thundering bricklayer. The one was gentleman born and bred and ever, in the fashion of the time, subscribed himself as such—but he failed at several forms of literature, gained but a few small successes, and then drifted into the obscurity of the medical profession and flitting recusancy. The other began in humbler wise, fought a path for his huge frame almost to the very door of the Mermaid, gained the ear of a literary king who came down out of Scotland in 1603, and as regular writer of court masques reveled in the gorgeous pageantry of nobility.

We do not know if the two ever met. We are aware of only two things they had in common, aside from their tastes for scribbling, namely, the remembrance of adventurous younger days and the experience of conversion. Because of this dissimilarity—a dissimilarity which, by the way, exists also in the very tenor of every line they wrote —it is only in our mind's eye that we can see them sitting together at some dusky London tavern, quaffing huge cups of malmsey or sack, making the very mullioned panes of those old windows shake with the roar of boisterous laughter, and seeing in the wraiths of smoke which drifted lazily up against the dark oaken beams—seeing such creatures, persons and places as never were on sea or land, as only their rare spirits could call down to earth. We find ourselves saying with wonderment, in the praises of Noyes:

> Souls of poets, dead and gone!
> What Elysium have ye known,
> Happy field, or mossy cavern,
> Choicer than the Mermaid Tavern?[1]

[1] From *Tales of the Mermaid Tavern* (1913), quoted with the permission of the publishers, Frederick A. Stokes Co., New York.

I

## Thomas Lodge

"Protogenes can know Apelles by his line though he see him not, and wise men can consider by the Penn of aucthorite of the writer though they know him not."—*Thos. Lodge.*

The usage of biography requires that I state at the outset that Thomas Lodge was born probably in 1556 or 1557, and died of the plague in 1625. Says Edmund Gosse:

"If a full and continuous biography of Thomas Lodge could be recovered, it would possess as much interest to a student of Elizabethan manners and letters as any memoir that can be imagined. It would combine, in a series of pictures, scenes from all the principal conditions of life in that stirring and vigorous age. It would introduce us to the stately civic life of London city, to Oxford in the early glow of humanism and liberal thought, to the dawn of the professional literature in London, to the life of a sailor on the high seas, to the poetry of the age, and then to its science, to the stage in London and to the anatomical lecture-room in Avignon, to the humdrum existence of a country practitioner, and to the perilous intrigues of a sympathizer with Catholicism trembling on the verge of treason."[2]

Such is usually the case of any man who makes a name, but not a great name, in the field of letters. The man of

---

[2] Edmund Gosse, *Seventeenth Century Studies*, p. 1. Quoted with the permission of Dodd, Mead and Co., publishers.

# Thomas Lodge

genius overcomes obstacles, blazes his own single trail and the world makes a path to his door. But he who is not so successful touches the life of his age in many ways. Thus in Defoe we find a truer reflection of his times than in Addison, in Southey a fuller landscape than in Byron, in Lodge a more typical view of Elizabethan days than in Shakespeare. The one is confined to letters, the other touches on nearly every phase of contemporary politics, commerce and thought. In one we get an idea; in the other ideas. And justly has Mr. Atkins said of Lodge: "His restless, unsettled career was typical of his age."[3]

It is almost characteristic of the spirit of colonization and the lure of scarce discovered lands that Lodge's first book defended something which did not yet exist. He had been to the Merchant Taylor's School, attended Trinity College at Oxford and was in residence in Lincoln's Inn, probably "eating his way to the bar," as the phrase goes, when Stephen Gosson issued *The School of Abuse* in 1579, attacking an evil which then scarcely existed, attacking even before it commenced, that great activity of heart and mind which has made memorable two words in all the English language—"Elizabethan Literature." There was a certain unforeseen justice in Lodge's answer: "No meruel though you disprayse poetrye, when you know not what it means! ... Them that have knowledge what comedies and tragedies be wil comend them, but it is sufferable in the folish to reprove that they know not." At any rate, Lodge was prompt in reply. We are ignorant as to the name of his

[3] This and succeeding quotations from Mr. Atkins, reprinted from his excellent chapter in Vol. III, *Cambridge History of English Literature*. By permission of The Macmillan Co., publishers.

tract, for the title pages of both existing copies are lost. We are ignorant of his motive, for though it was charged that the players advertised for a supporter to their cause, there is no certainty as to why Lodge in particular took up the gauntlet. But take up the gauntlet he did, and in no uncertain or delicate terms assailed the Puritan. He told Gosson that that Puritan was trying to raise up a new set of unnatural stoics, that he had forgotten his learning since leaving college, and that he never gained proper instruction from his reading. Lodge defended literature on somewhat the same grounds as Sidney. "A heavenly, a perfect gift," says Lodge. "To teach and delight," added Sidney. Lodge's pamphlet, though not comparable to Sidney's fine philosophical study, yet deserves credit for being the first in the field.

But it is noteworthy that Lodge can point with pride to no British publication and has to be content with mentioning the classics as proof of his contention. His next care was to produce what he had praised. Records for these years are very scant, but we at least know that in 1584 he produced an *Alarum Against Usurers*, a tract somewhat of the type we usually associate with Dekker, and in 1589 *Scilla's Metamorphosis*, a classical poem in the decorative manner of romance. In the latter he declares his intention

> To write no more of that whence shame doth grow
> Or tie my pen to penning knaves' delight,
> But live with fame and so for fame to write.

Scholars have been inclined to interpret this as a decision to abandon all dramatic writing, but there is doubt as to

*Thomas Lodge*

whether or what he had written in a dramatic vein before. We do at least know that he associated no longer with cheap scribblers, but rather with Daniel and Drayton, and then took himself far afield.

Lodge's next published work was his most famous *Rosalynde*, 1590. Significantly he says in his preface "to the gentleman readers":

"Room for a soldier and a sailor, that gives you the fruits of his labors that he wrote in the ocean, when every line was wet with a surge and every humorous passion counter-checked with a storm. If you like it, so; and yet I will be yours in duty if you be mine in favor. But if Momus or any squint-eyed ass that hath mighty ears to conceive with Midas, and yet little reason to judge, if he came aboard our bark to find fault with the tackling, when he knows not the shrouds, I'll down into the hold and fetch out a rusty pole-axe that saw no sun this seven year, and either well baste him or heave the cockscomb overboard to feed cods."

This was the spirit of an adventurer who heard the winds and the waves roar, who boarded a Spanish galleon with as light a heart as he cribbed stanzas from any French or Italian book. No mere chance led this young man on the seas abroad. It was the spirit of the age. And his discoveries were not merely reckoned in peoples and lands or Spanish doubloons. He sailed, about 1588, for the Azores and the Canaries, where, perhaps under the very guns of Angra, he wrote this prose romance, modeling partly after the pseudo-Chaucerian "Tale of Gamelyn" and partly after his own fancy, but modeling so well that Shakespeare was content to adopt it almost unaltered for the immortal plot of *As You Like It*. Says Mr. Grey: "It has been treated merely as a source, as a thing of no value in itself; the interest it has aroused has been antiquarian rather than literary." But there are situations in it which are unforgettable: Where Rosader woos Rosalynde in the person of Ganymede in a courtly and courteous style the world has unhappily long forgotten, where Rosader saves from a lion the brother who has done him wrong, where Rosader refuses aid and nourishment until his old and feeble friend Adam is properly relieved. The style is after the balanced manner of Lyly —rhetorical, allusive, figurative, conventional. And this influence of the author of *Euphues* is seen in the very subtitle of Lodge's book, "Euphues' Golden Legacie"; it is seen in passages of *The Wounds of Civil War, A Lookingglass for London and England; The Life and Death of William Longbeard*, particularly in the romance *Euphues' Shadow*, sent from America and pushed through the press in 1592 by poor, unfortunate Robert Greene. Whether this imitation of the courtly phrase of Lyly was due to a probable personal connection at Oxford, or to the prevailing mode of the time, it is difficult to determine. But it matters little. There are passages in *Rosalynde* that have an undying charm. When Sir John of Bordeaux bids farewell to his sons, there are sentiments as fine and almost as well expressed as the advice of Polonius to Laertes. This personal romance in prose, which incidentally has nothing at all to do with the sea, may stand on its own worth—not very high, perhaps, but yet high enough to be read, admired, and loved for many generations to come.

It is not true, as Mr. Atkins has said of *Rosalynde*, that in Lodge's next important work, "environment worked only by contrast." *Phillis* (1595) was indeed "hatched in the storms of the ocean and feathered in the surges of many perilous seas."[4] In *Rosalynde* there were pastoral fields instead of sea waves, but in *Phillis*—one of those curious sonnet sequences so popular in the last decade of the sixteenth century—there are references aplenty to "the wat'ry world, where now I sail." For these delicate complimentary songs, surpassed only by the charming lyrics which dot the letter-press of *Rosalynde*, are never far from "the wrestling waves." Sea nymphs are under the bow and Cupid is at the helm. The poems were written on another adventurous expedition into waters ruled by proud Castile and lordly Aragon, when Lodge shipped with the great seaman Cavendish to South America, Brazil, and even the Straits of Magellan. They were written in the pastoral vein, to a shepherdess at home tending her flocks on gentle slopes; but they do not completely forget, in their imagery, the rush of water past the ship or the hiss of a foaming wake. They are neither pure pastorals nor pure piscatories. They blend the two. One is an elegy at parting, when

> The winds are fair, the sails are hoisted high,
> The anchors weighed.

Another, Sonnet XI, is entirely and completely concerned with the imagery of sea scenes:

> My frail and earthly bark, by reason's guide,
> Which holds the helm, whilst will doth wield the sail,
> By my desires, the winds of bad betide,
> Hath sailed these worldly seas with small avail,
> Vain objects serve for dreadful rocks to quail

[4] Lodge, in the dedication to *Rosalynde*.

> My brittle boat from haven of life that flies
> To haunt the sea of mundane miseries.
> My soul that draws impressions from above,
> And views my course, and sees the winds aspire,
> Bids reason watch to 'scape the shoals of love;
> But lawless will enflamed with endless ire
> Doth steer em poop, whilst reason doth retire.
> The streams increase; love's waves my bark do fill;
> Thus are they wracked that guide their course by will.

Mr. Atkins cannot here say that environment worked only by contrast, or Miss Crow that "as far as the imagery of the sonnets is concerned, the pageantry of day and night at sea might have passed before blinded eyes!"[5]

To continue the figure, Lodge was not blind to the beauties of the sea nor—as the very penetrating gaze of Sir Sidney Lee has discovered—was he blind to the beauties of other literatures. He casually joined a plundering expedition to South America and just as casually played the freebooter among the poems of Petrarch, Ronsard, Ariosto, Sanazzara, Bembo, Paschale and Desportes. Sir Sidney Lee has traced eighteen out of the thirty-four poems in *Phillis* to foreign sources, and says finally of Lodge: "He merits the first place among Elizabethan plagiarists."[6] And, in extenuation, all we can say is that when other men pillaged at sea, so did Lodge; when other men stole Continental meters and concepts in literature, so did Lodge.

If literary men of those Elizabethan times especially were particularly prone to borrowing foreign forms and

---

[5] *Elizabethan Sonnet Cycles, Philis-Licia*, London, 1896, p. 18.
[6] *Cambridge History of English Literature*, Vol. III, p. 298. By permission of The Macmillan Co., publishers.

phrases, the same can scarcely be said of the dramatists. A reckless and irresponsible crew they were indeed, but the predecessors of Shakespeare molded a new form and created a new method and purpose on the stage. The fall of princes, the virtue of ladies, the value of courage, the clash of conflicting wills—these were subjects which in a British theater brought to their toes groundlings who were already on their feet. Lodge touched but slightly the moods of the playwrights. *The Wounds of Civil War* and *A Looking-glass for London and England* were probably both presented while he was absent from England, and, though our evidence in this, as in other matters concerning Elizabethan drama, is very scant, it was probably his friend Robert Greene, "Maister in Arts," who saw them on the stage. We are not sure when they were produced—possibly before the *Scilla's Metamorphosis* (1589) mentioned above, certainly before 1594, when they were both printed. It is also probable that of many other pieces attributed to him, *A Larum for London*, not printed until 1602, was also by Lodge. These form the total of his productive work in that field of the drama for which he wrote his premature defense in 1570, and the *Looking-glass* was a collaboration play, written with Greene. None of the plays is good. *A Larum for London* is the least distinguished; *The Wounds of Civil War*, founded on that Plutarch which Shakespeare had to use in translation, has the best plot, and *A Looking-glass for London and England*, telling of the sins of Nineveh,[7] has the best scenes. These last two show undoubted influences of Marlowe:

[7] Cf. The "motions," puppet show of Nineveh, mentioned in *Every Man Out of His Humour*, Act II., scene 1.

> I'll make her streets, that peer into the clouds,
> Burnish'd with gold and ivory pillars fair,
> Shining with jasper, jet and ebony,
> All like the palace of the morning sun,
> To swim within a sea of purple blood,
> Before I lose the name of general[8]

and "Six hundred towers that topless touch the clouds,"[9] and an impassioned scene on the dire distress that shall fall on Nineveh,[10] and a repetitious declamation:

> Come, lads, though Rasin wants his Ragadon,
> Earth will repay him many Ragadons,
> And Alinda with pleasant looks revive
> The heart that droupes for want of Ragadon—

all these remind us of him who reached so high and fell so low—Marlowe. But even these tales of wars in Flanders, civil strife in Rome and apocalyptic dominations are never far from Lodge's own British town. There are humble scenes—menials who speak Londonese, "jolly stuff," drinkings, beatings, rollicking sons, social satire on deceitful lawyers and usurious knaves; and all these scenes are really in Cheapside or Southwark. It was no mere chance that Lodge wrote so well[11] "the tidings full of wonder and amaze." Says the rubric, "Enter the merchant of Tharsus,

---

[8] *The Wounds of Civil War*, Act I., scene 1.
[9] *A Looking-glass for London and England*, Act I., Scene 1, cf. Marlowe: "The Topless Towers of Illium."
[10] Differs in final resolution from the final scene of *Dr. Faustus*.
[11] Assuming that he wrote it, not Greene, for we have eschewed what Mr. Saintsbury calls "the fruitless and always uncertain task of separation."

# Thomas Lodge

the M. of the ship, some sailors wet from the sea," and then follows a description of a storm at sea. Not from the city of St. Paul did Lodge get his material, nor even from Holy Scripture. He got it himself on one of these voyages made in the company of adventurous British seamen.[12] And yet, except for some few such purple patches as these, there is nothing distinctive or distinguished in his dramatic work. In the words of Collier, "One of his original pieces [which were very few] made melancholy reference to his want of success in different spheres of life, and especially in connection with the stage."[13] So, to quote again, "Lodge, at best a wayfarer in the hostel of the drama, made way for a throng of inpouring enthusiasts—and made way contemptuously."[14]

The last thirty years of Lodge's life, from 1595 to 1625, are the most interesting and the least studied. They are also the years with which recent research has least concerned itself, and it is probably to them that future scholars will turn, not so much for material illustrative of the drama as for insight into the purely personal activities of a declining age. In 1600, we are told, Lodge took a medical degree at Avignon and in 1602 was incorporated as "Doctor of Physic" in the University of Oxford. He had little to do with the theater, though he was probably friendly with Dekker, and he devoted himself to his profession and to translation of serious tomes from foreign languages. There are, in the documents of that period which have survived

---

[12] In one of his pamphlets Lodge tells "Of maine famous pirats, who in times past were Lordes of the Sea."
[13] J. P. Collier in introduction to an edition of *William Longbeard*.
[14] Professor G. P. Baker in *Cambridge History of English Literature*, Vol. V., p. 157.

the wear of time and the misuse of libraries, occasional references to him as a medical man, and Mr. Gosse has unearthed a letter which indicates that Lodge was active in Catholic circles in years when such activity was unpopular, if not dangerous. For Lodge had definitely gone over to Rome.

In years when British materialism was almost synonymous with ardent Protestantism, Lodge had forgotten the religious differences which sharpened the Armada conflict into an almost sectarian warfare. In his *Life of Robin the Devil* (1591) he had shown an evident sympathy for Roman forms of worship.[15] In *A Larum for London* (1594-1602) he assails "the swelling pride and tyrannie of Spaine" and yet makes no attack on religious grounds, although a priory, a convent and the Mass are casually mentioned. In *The Life and Death of William Longbeard* (1593), though there is a dissembling "Abbot of Cadonence in Normandie," Lodge tells of a pope who overcomes a wicked pirate, speaks of a queen building a church in honor of Our Lady, and elsewhere refers in decorous words to the Blessed Virgin. This tendency is all the more noteworthy when we find him on that expedition with Cavendish in 1592 reading from a library of the fathers in a college of Jesuits at Santos. We are delightfully reminded, as we think of Lodge bending over those old books, of the words of Cicero in the oration in defense of Archias, the poet, where he remarks that these studies and tastes for literature are of all times and of all

---

[15] There was nothing remarkable in the priest solemnizing the marriage of Rosader and Rosalynde. Even Spenser used the word "priest" without resentment in *The Shepherdes Calender*.

places, and then goes on to say, "*Pernoctant nobiscum, peregrinantur, rusticantur.*"¹⁶

Perchance this inclination toward a familiarity with Catholicism was the chiefest treasure Lodge brought back with him from that expedition—we know of no other that he brought. The faint touch of Catholicism evident in *The Devil Conjured* (1596) and *Wit's Misery* (1596) is strengthened and deeply confirmed in a religious tract, *Prosopoeia; or, Tears of the Holy, Blessed and Sanctified Mary, the Mother of God*, published in 1596. By 1623¹⁷ he was able to write of these things in the tone of secure acceptance. And the reason for all this lies probably in his second marriage, about the year 1596, with a Mrs. Jane Albridge (or Aldred), a Catholic widow, who was formerly a dependent of Lodge's early patron, Sir Francis Walsingham, and who had established a wide reputation for herself as an active recusant.

So with a growing practice and an increasing professional reputation, Thomas Lodge ended his days in communion with the Holy See at Rome. He had tried to win a reputation at many things, stooped to scurrilous pamphleteering, traveled across the seas as a freebooter, wrote some bad plays, penned a series of exquisite sonnets, contributed one splendid prose romance to increase the glory of Elizabethan literature, and finally turned in middle life to a new profession and to a new faith. Whether all his efforts and

---
[16] Quoted by Lodge in his *Defense of Poetry* in 1579. From Cicero, of course, in his oration on the poet Archias where he says of literary studies: "They are with us through the night, travel with us, go even into the country with us."

[17] *The Poor Man's Talent* (1623).

all his journeys were worth the labor, whether all his polemics, his poetry and his plays brought him any satisfaction, it is not for us to say. Lost in the records of the past are the many personal details which went to make up the daily life of a man who emerged but now and then into the public prints. At all events, he has left us something to charm our reading hours; and across the page sways and sweeps the shadow of his curious and many-sided personality. With Keats we can only wonder and hazard the query:

> Bards of Passion and of Mirth!
> Ye have left your souls on earth.
> Have ye souls in heaven, too,
> Double-lived in regions new?

II

## Ben Jonson

The second of our Elizabethans, Ben Jonson, was born in 1573 and died in 1637, and his best work for the stage was done between 1598 and 1614, after Lodge had retired. Like the great Samuel Johnson of a century and a half later, he himself is more interesting than anything he ever wrote. He of all men is the person who made the Mermaid Tavern famous:

> There, flitting to and fro with cups of wine,
> I heard them toss the Chrysomelean names
> From mouth to mouth—Lyly and Peale and Lodge,
> Kit Marlowe, Michael Drayton, and the rest,
> With Ben, rare Ben, bricklayer Ben, who rolled

# Ben Jonson

>     Like a giant galleon on his ingle-bench.
>     Some twenty years of age he seemed: and yet
>     This huge Gargantua with the bulldog jaws,
>     The T, for Tyburn, branded on his thumb,
>     And grim pock-pitted face, was growling tales
>     To Dekker that would fright a buccaneer—
>     How in the fierce Low Countries he had killed
>     His man, and won that scar on his bronzed fist;
>     Was taken prisoner, and turned Catholick;
>     And, now returned to London, was resolved
>     To blast away the vapours of the town
>     With Boreas-throated plays of thunderous mirth.
>     "I'll thwack their tribulation-wholesomes,[18] lad,
>     Their Yellow-faced Envies and lean Thorns-i'-the-Flesh."[19]

In other words, he was a man with what might be called a roaring personality. He was a fighter. He had fought on the battlefield for certain principles and now was disposed to fight on the stage for other principles. His most famous character, Captain Bobadill, a first study for Falstaff, boasts of having completed a single combat in the face of the army,[20] but Jonson had actually done the thing himself.

"In his service in the Low Countries he had, in the face of both the campes, killed ane enemie and taken *opima spolia* from him."[21]

---

[18] "Tribulation Wholesome, a pastor of Amsterdam," is a character in *The Alchemist*, and will be mentioned later. In Shakespeare's *Henry VIII* (Act V., Scene 3) there is a reference to the Tribulation of Tower Hill, which evidently means the meeting of some particular set of Puritans.

[19] From *Tales of the Mermaid Tavern*, by Alfred Noyes. Copyright, 1913, quoted by permission of Frederick A. Stokes Co., publishers.

[20] *Every Man in His Humour*, Act IV., Scene 5.

[21] *Conversations with William Drummond*, the Shakespeare Society, 1842, a valuable source for biographical material. Hereafter referred to as *Drummond*.

And he likewise had boasted of his deed in the epigram "To True Soldiers":

> I swear by you, true friend, my Muse, I love
> Your great profession, which I once did prove;
> And did not shame it with my actions then,
> No more than I dare now do with my pen.

After returning to England, "being appealed to the fields, he had killed his adversarie, which had hurt him in the arme, and whose sword was larger than his, for the which he was emprissoned, and almost at the gallows."[22] Again he got into a fight, though the killing of this Gabriel Spenser would seem to have been serious enough to have been a warning. "He had many quarrells with Marston, beat him, and took his pistol from him."[23] And he demonstrated his courage in another way when this same Marston and Chapman, with both of whom he had collaborated on *Eastward Hoe!* were imprisoned for some sentiments contained in that play. Jonson forthwith marched into the jail and declared that he would share their punishment. Finally, Jonson even quarreled with the renowned architect, Inigo Jones, to whom he was under obligations, if he did not actually owe him for bread and butter. But this quarrel was more of the quill and ink honor than of the pistol and powder box. Jonson wrote, condemning, though he feigned to overlook:

> Thy forehead is too narrow for my brand.

[22] *Drummond.*
[23] *Drummond.*

This thundering person was ever in the thick of what we now call "the war of the theaters," for he had set out in the very beginning to be a reformer. Though his comedies frequently did not pay for fire and doorkeeper in the theater,[24] and "off all his playes he never gained two hundreth pounds,"[25] he had the courage to maintain his principles in the face of failure. There were two great dramatic reformers of this age, one a romantic, the other a realist. There was Marlowe, who said:

> From jigging veins of rhyming mother wits
> And such conceits as clownage keeps in pay,
> We lead you to the stately tents of war.

There was Jonson, ten years later, who said he would give

> Deeds and language, such as men do use,
> And persons, such as comedy would choose,
> When she would show an image of the times,
> And sport with human follies, not with crimes.

He thought the formlessness of the English drama deplorable and its violation of the unities outrageous. He despised the unnatural wars, the bombastic rhetoric and the political intrigue—on the stage. "These paper pedlars! these ink-dabblers! . . . are the most shallow, pitiful, barren fellows that live upon the face of the earth." He believed, as Ludovic Halévy has since stated, that "the drama is not the land of chimeras and fantasy, it is one of the exact

---

[24] Gervinius, *Shakespeare Commentaries*.
[25] *Drummond*.

sciences"; and let slip no occasion to criticize those who violated the ancient principles by which alone he deemed perfection could be attained. "The rough and rugged one," he called a character who was supposed to represent himself, and there was little of the smoothness of old-time culture in his violent criticisms.

As early as 1598 he condemned *Hieronimo Is Mad Again!* —an old play which needed condemnation. In 1599 he was supposed to be ridiculing Marston and Dekker, and in *The Poetaster* (1601) he attacked them openly. In *Cynthia's Revels* (1600) he laughed at Marston and the Euphuists and raved against pastoral conventions.[26] In *Every Man Out of His Humour* he made fun of platonic love as it appeared in the sonnets. Small wonder, then, that Mr. Herford has called criticism "the dominant habit of Jonson's mind." There is nothing accidental in this writing of Jonson's, none of the dilettantism which crops up from time to time in Lodge. He wrote a splendid appreciation of the role poetry should play, which unfortunately appeared only in the first edition of *Every Man in His Humour*. And he wished to exalt "the despised head of poetry again, and strip her out of those rotten and base rags wherein the times have adulterated her form."[27] His theory he sought to sustain by hard work and determination, and it sometimes chanced that his theory overshadowed his genius.

Nor was his witticism confined to literary topics. In those diverging days of Elizabeth men went

---

[26] Tieck thinks that the closing lines of the epilogue of this play furnished Shakespeare with the title of *As You Like It*.
[27] Dedication to *Volpone, or The Fox*.

> To see the wonders of the world abroad, ...
> Some to the wars, to try their fortunes there;
> Some to discover islands far away,
> Some to the studious universities.

Ben Jonson cared not if they went abroad, but he would have them return home as good Englishmen as when they left. He stood for solid nationalism, a center about which the growing Empire might revolve. But he had no use for fashions imported from other lands—for the affectation of the "Englishman Italianate," for the insincerity of the religious fanatics from Holland, for the fripperies which the gallant brought home from Paris.

> With an armed and resolved hand
> I'll strip the ragged follies of the time.[28]

It is social witticism of a keen and piercing kind which gives a unity and a purpose to his writing that enables us to put him beside Langland and Malory, Chaucer and Thomas More, as a man who writes not only for his own time, but for all time; not only for all time, but directly for his own.[29]

Jonson knew the Elizabethan age as only that man knows who has tried its adventures and undergone its hardships. This man whom critics have tried to identify with Shakespeare's Ajax, "the mongrel, beef-witted lord,"[30] was

---

[28] It is significant that Jonson gives English characters to the Italian plot on which he built the play *Every Man in His Humour*.

[29] A case in point refers to the practice of gallants sitting upon the very stage. Yet *The Gull's Horn Book* and *The Old Wive's Tale* usually mentioned in this connection, do not illustrate the practice better than Jonson's *Every Man Out of His Humour* and *Cynthia's Revels*.

[30] See *Troilus and Cressida*, Act I., Scene 2, ll. 19–32.

"brought up poorly, put to school by a friend, after taken from it, and put to one other craft"; yet "he was better versed and knew more in Greek and Latin than all the poets in England." "The trade of bricklayer could bring no such distinction as that of letters; and aside from becoming official masque writer to King James, he was finally made Master of Arts in both the universities, by their favor, not his studies."[81] He had literally to struggle forward, even sometimes having violent disagreements with those who were "sealed of the tribe of Ben." If he was "given rather to loose a friend than a jest," his companions were no less careful of his feelings. One of them wrote for him an epitaph which Jonson good-naturedly communicated to Drummond:

> Here lyes Benjamin Johnson dead,
> And hath no more wit than [a] goose in his head;
> That as he was wont, so doth he still,
> Live by his wit and evermore will.

And sometimes his living was not so easy. We have already mentioned the small sum he said he received from his comedies. It was true, of course, that "every first day of the new year he had twenty pounds sent him from the Earl of Pembroke to buy bookes."[82] It was true that he can in a sense be called the first poet laureate, because he received a regular "pension" in the form of a barrel of wine. But even the wine was not delivered punctually and he had, at least once, to write a rebuke to the royal authorities.

[81] These three quotations from *Drummond*.
[82] *Drummond*.

> What can the cause be, when the King hath given
> His poet sack, the Household will not pay?

But there was one thing in Ben Jonson's life which was probably a more dangerous adventure than any "war of the theaters" or actual battle in the field. He told Drummond that when he was in prison he embraced a new religion; and though he perhaps did not embrace it very ardently, it was at least risky to be on speaking terms with Catholicism.

"Then [1598] took he his religion by trust, of a priest who visited him in prisson. Thereafter he was twelve yeares a Papist. . . . After he was reconciled with the Church, and left of to be a recusant, at his first Communion, in token of true reconciliation, he drank out all the full cup of wine."[33]

It shall not be our purpose here, as some Catholic writers have done, to gloat over his conversion, to elaborate unnecessarily on all too scanty details, or to speak of his later return to Anglicanism as a "shameful apostasy." There is too much impassioned intolerance put to paper already. Suffice it to remark that by Northampton he was "accused of Poperie and treason" for his *Sejanus* (1603), and that we must not forget the words "by trust." Speaking of this qualifying admission, Mr. Herford has spoken quite sensibly:

"It would be rash to assert, in the face of this phrase, that his conviction was very profound, or that it was reached by a very elaborate process of reasoning. But it is still more out of the question to treat it as a mere whim. The heresy

---

[33] *Drummond.*

which he had embraced in prison when in the very grasp of the Queen's Government and danger of his life, he retained for twelve years among the more subtle temptations of Court favor; and had recusancy been a safer and easier game than it was, the sterling honesty of Jonson is wholly above suspicion. He is entitled to the credit of equal sincerity when he took his first sacrament in prison bread, and when, a dozen years later, he characteristically drained the cup 'in token of true reconciliation.' At the same time the sturdy heroism involved in recusancy under Elizabeth may well have had a certain attraction for this soldier among poets, who, without courting the role of Ishmael, played it, when forced upon him, with a certain grim zest. And it may be suggested also that the most ancient of living forms of Christianity appealed powerfully to the scholar Jonson, whose 'humble gleanings in divinity after the fathers' were long afterwards among the ruined treasures of his study.'[34]

And we know that he condemns Presbyterianism in *A Tale of a Tub*. He attacks Puritans in *Bartholomew Fair*, particularly Zeal-of-the-Land Busy, formerly a baker, who dreams now and sees visions, and ridicules in *The Alchemist* those who "whine of purity and hypocrisy." It was not safe then, when the Puritan middle class was gathering strength for the great rebellion, to say of them: *Dum vitant stultitia, in contraria currunt*,[35] or to speak as follows to a pastor of Amsterdam and Ananias, his deacon:

---

[34] From the introduction to the Mermaid edition, p. xxi.
[35] "When fools avoid faults they rush into opposite extremes."

> Call yourselves
> By names of Tribulation, Persecution,
> Restraint, Long-patience, and such-like, affected
> By the whole family or mood of you,
> Only for glory, and to catch the ear
> Of the disciple.[36]

In *Bartholomew Fair* (1614)—and the date is important, because it was after Jonson had returned to Anglicanism—he inserts among other ridiculous statements from the lips of Zeal-of-the-Land Busy, a condemnation of "those superstitious relics, those lists of Latin, the very rags of Rome, and patches of Popery." (The surrounding context is significant.) In *Every Man in His Humour* (1598) he commends a rigid Roman Catholic who stands by his oath; there is *The Ghyrland of the Blessed Virgin Marie* (1635), which has been attributed to him; in *Volpone, or the Fox* (1605) he has a decent reference to a good Catholic; and though he does allow himself to tell Drummond a joke on a Catholic king, he more than compensates by saying to the same man of Hawthornden:

> That Southwell was hanged (in 1595); yet so he had written that piece of his, the "Burning Babe," he would have been content to have destroyed many of his.

But it is silly to try to quarrel over the religious beliefs of these men.

Ben Jonson in his work and in his influence has left an imperishable heritage. To them we should direct attention. His work is many-sided. *Sejanus* (1603) is a Roman tragedy

---

[36] *The Alchemist*, Act III, Scene 2.

worthy of Shakespeare. His *Explorata, or Discoveries*, were equal, if not superior, to the famous *Essays of Francis Bacon*,[37] and led Swinburne to say, "A fool may talk, but a wise man speaks." He has been given by scholars a rollicking ballad in Percy's *Reliques* called "The Merry Pranks of Robin Goodfellow." His classical learning underlies all his work[38] and bring us some apt, though not exact, translations from Horace and Martial. Coleridge remarks that *The Alchemist* has one of the three most perfect plots ever planned, and Dryden that *The Silent Woman* represents the highest perfection of dramatic art on record. Says Swinburne: "Not even the ardor of his most fanciful worshippers, from the data of Cartwright and Randolph to the data of Gilchrist and Pifford, could exaggerate the actual greatness of his various and marvelous energies."[39]

In his plays he set a new fashion. He tried to abide by the unities. He took into full consideration the difficulties of actual stage representation,[40] and yet, with the possible exception of Shakespeare, he was less contaminated with the clamor of popular wish than any other dramatist of his time. He had a scholar's ideas of what was right and wrong, and therefore composed his plays to fit those ideas, not to fit the public—which was therefore less pleased with them. Where Shakespeare chose what he thought fitting and welded all together, Jonson vigorously rejected what he

---

[37] Much credit must be given Jonson for his high praise in these *Discoveries*, as also in *Underwoods*, for the disgraced Lord Vauclain.

[38] Even *Every Man Out of His Humour*.

[39] To this Swinburne says: "Il maestro di color che sanno."

[40] For instance, he tells Drummond that "he had an intention to have made a play like 'Plautus Amphitrio,' but left it off, for that he could never find so two like others that he could persuade the spectators they were one."

deemed unfitting and kept the remainder. The artistic results were not far different from a technical point of view; but the modes of work were quite contrary. The product in both cases bore the undisputed marks of genius.

Now at the end of this essay we shall put three quotations from Ben Jonson which in a way summarize his difficulties, his ideals and his enduring charm. Not only that. They typify the same things and could be applied to almost any worthy writer of the age of Elizabeth.

First, as to his critics against whom he fought:

> At last they would object to me my poverty: I confess she is my domestic; sober of diet, simple of habit, frugal, painful, a good counsellor to me, that keeps me from cruelty, pride or other more delicate impertinences, which are the nurse-children of riches.

Second, as to his ideal and aim:

> Indeed if you will look on poesy
> As she appears to many, poor and lame,
> Patch'd up in remnants and old worn-out rags,
> Half-starved for want of her peculiar food,
> Sacred invention; then I must confirm
> Both your conceit and censure of her merit;
> But view her in her glorious ornaments,
> Attired in the majesty of art,
> Set high in spirit with the precious taste
> Of sweet philosophy; and, which is most,
> Crowned with the rich traditions of a soul
> That hates to have her dignity profaned
> With any relish of an earthly thought,
> Oh, then, how proud a presence doth she bear!

The third and last is his just appeal to the modern reader as well as to him of old time:

> Only vouchsafe me your attentions
> And I will give you music worth your ears.

That was Ben Jonson—and that was the spirit of the Elizabethan dramatists, men of learning and men of wit, who transfigured the English stage.

# 6

## Shakespeare and Catholicism

ON THE religion of Shakespeare much has been written,[1] but little that is conclusive. For although we know more, perhaps, about Shakespeare himself than about any other dramatist of his time, we still know so little and have to conjecture so much that the usual result of such inquiries will be merely, words, words, words.

That he altered several of the old plays from which he drew source material for his own productions proves little or nothing beyond the greatness of his art. The omission of violent partisan statements from *King John* and *Romeo and Juliet* was not the act of a dissenter from the Established Church so much as it was the act of a man who knew that partisan statements appeal to a few, and nonpartisan statements may find favor with all. Then when we find the machinery of a particular faith in a play whose scene is laid in a Catholic country or in Catholic times, our only assumption is that these things are in character. Others will

[1] *The Bible in Shakespeare*, by William Burgess, New York, 1903; *The Religion of Shakespeare*, by H. S. Bowden, London, 1899; "The Religion of Shakespeare," by Edward R. Russell, *The Theological Review*, October, 1876; *Shakespeare's Stellung zur Katholischen Religion*, by J. M. Raich, Mainz, 1884; "Was Shakespeare a Catholic?" by James J. Walsh, *The Catholic Mind*, 22 April, 1915; and Herbert Thurston, S.J. (who seems to have kept his head better than most of the others), in the article on Shakespeare in *The Catholic Encyclopedia* and in *America*, 22 April, 1916.

point out the essential similarities between Shakespeare's statements and Catholicism, and the great differences between these same statements and "modern ethical teachers," "prevailing widespread pessimism," and "Puritan self-complacency," forgetting that Elizabethan England had very nearly the same religious faith, though not the same religious allegiance, as the Catholic countries.

On the whole, the soundest scholars are agreed that any Catholic hypothesis in this matter is founded on very scant ground, for which there seems to be ample contradictory evidence. It were vain to attempt to establish and carry out such an argument. If, finally, we are able to say that Shakespeare "in a special way belongs to us" and to write Q. E. D. at the end, it seems that Catholics would for some time after be engaged in blushing for many of his passages, and in explaining them away by many devious turns of scholastic logic. We cannot, you know, claim as Shakespeare's own thought those sentiments with which we agree and relegate as merely "in character" those which we find un-Catholic. Because Shakespeare was a dramatist, his characters speak, himself never.

The proper way to consider the whole body of Shakespeare's writing, if we must write of him from the Catholic viewpoint, is to consider his plays objectively. They are fiction on the stage or they are history on the stage. And we must simply look upon them as they have come down to us after three-hundred-odd years as fiction and as history. In this and the following chapter we shall then make some slight study of the works of William Shakespeare, and consider them as food for the modern reader who wants a criticism from one of his own faith on such passages as

# Shakespeare and Catholicism

refer to matters of religion, taking first the historical plays, and later those plays which may be termed fiction.

I

The historical plays of Shakespeare, with the years to which they refer, are as follows:[2]

| Name of Play | Kingship | Date of Play |
|---|---|---|
| King John | 1199–1216 | 1593 |
| Richard II | 1377–1399 | 1595 |
| I Henry IV | 1399– | 1597 |
| II Henry IV | –1413 | 1598 |
| Henry V | 1413–1422 | 1599 |
| I Henry VI | 1422– | 1590–1 |
| II Henry VI | — | 1590–2 |
| III Henry VI | –1461 | 1590–2 |
| Richard III | 1483–1485 | 1593 |
| Henry VIII | 1509–1547 | 1612 |

The first of these plays deals with a king and a reign when religion was a bitter contention of political import. King John was historically on both sides of the fence. He opposed Rome and he was befriended by Rome; and his reputation in all matters is far from spotless.

We must listen with caution to the ecclesiastical chroniclers in the case of a king who quarrelled with the Church. Yet they do not seem to have gone much beyond the mark

[2] The dates are taken from the excellent introductions in *The Tudor Shakespeare* and from *The Facts about Shakespeare* (New York: The Macmillan Co., 1913), with the permission of the publishers.

in saying that John when he died made hell fouler by his coming. His throne of cruelty, lust, perfidy, and rapine was upheld by mercenary troops, the scourge of a nation.[3]

In spite of his many bad actions, the reign of John accomplished two good things for England: the loss of Normandy with its resulting increase of nationalism, and the grant of Magna Charta at the command of those northern lords and barons who were thoroughly English in all their origins and purposes. In spite of John's usurpation of the throne, his lack of principle, and his antagonism to certain chartered liberties, the play which served as the basis for Shakespeare's drama, *The Troublesome Raigne of John King of England*, printed in 1591,[4] upholds his scandalous proceedings and it is not without profit to notice a few of the points in which Shakespeare's version differs from the older one. Says Thorndike:

> Perhaps the most significant single change Shakespeare made was the excision of the anti-Romanist bias which in the older play had made John a Protestant hero.[5]

Falconbridge ransacking the churches, the stabbing of an abbot, scenes from the old play, are omitted by Shakespeare. John was not a Protestant, of course; for, though he

---

[3] *The United Kingdom. A Political History.* By Goldwin Smith (New York, 1899), pp. 118-119. I have intentionally quoted here and elsewhere, from a historical writer who very evidently has a cumulative dislike for the Catholic Church. Quotations made by permission of the Macmillan Co., publishers.

[4] This is supposed to have been written during the year of the Armada, and often acted.

[5] *The Facts about Shakespeare*, p. 78.

opposed the Pope on one occasion and so called down upon himself and his kingdom excommunication and the interdict, it must not be forgotten that John appealed to Rome to stop the later French invasion, that a papal legate sat by his side at Runnymede in opposition to those rebellious barons who named themselves the Army of God and Holy Church, nor that the Pope himself, now friendly to John, condemned the Charter as an ungrateful outrage. In admitting the spiritual and denying the temporal supremacy of the Holy See in English affairs, John was no more a Protestant than was Sir Thomas More, who died "in and for the faith of the holy Catholic Church,"[6] maintaining the same distinction.

Having shorn "that usurping John"[7] of Protestant qualities, Shakespeare next proceeded to take from him the heroic. Constance of Bretagne was really remarried at the time of the action of the play, but Shakespeare lets her remain a persecuted widow with a persecuted son, and by thus gaining a brilliant dramatic conflict of characters as well as of forces, appeals to our sympathies for both Constance and Arthur and makes John appear more cruel and ruthless than the earlier play had done. John's actual ordering of the death of the rightful claimant, Arthur, and his hypocritical change of sentiment on the subject, are likewise new scenes introduced by Shakespeare. The source play would have us believe that the man was preferred to the boy; but Shakespeare emphasizes the fact that John acts in his "strong possession much more than his right."[8]

[6] Roper's *Life of More*, closing paragraph.
[7] Shakespeare, *King John*, Act III, Scene 1, line 61.
[8] *Ibid.*, Act I, Scene 1, line 40.

Again Shakespeare condenses John's four wars into two so as to make it seem that one turned entirely about the question of Arthur's title, and the other Arthur's death, bringing the boy heir into an unwarranted prominence and confining the ecclesiastical controversies to unimportant positions.

Thus, by heightening the character of Arthur and suppressing virulent religious prejudice, Shakespeare has written a play which appeals to the human heart direct, of the Elizabethan age and of our own. The protests against papal political interference from "a royal criminal, weak in his criminality,"[9] who wishes to "shake the bags of hoarding abbots,"[10] are political protests and nothing more. They are not directed against a religious faith.

*Enter* PANDULPH.

*King Philip.* Here comes the holy legate of the Pope.
*Pandulph.* Hail, you anointed deputies of heaven!
To Thee, King John, my holy errand is.
I, Pandulph, of fair Milan cardinal,
And from Pope Innocent the legate here,
Do in his name religiously demand
Why thou against the Church, our holy mother,
So wilfully dost spurn, and force perforce
Keep Stephen Langton, chosen Archbishop
Of Canterbury, from that holy see?
This, in our foresaid holy father's name,
Pope Innocent, I do demand of thee.
*King John.* What earthly name to interrogatories

[9] Dowden.
[10] Shakespeare, *King John*, Act III, Scene III, lines 7–8.

>                   Can task the free breath of a sacred king?
>                   Thou canst not, Cardinal, devise a name
>                   So slight, unworthy, and ridiculous,
>                   To charge me to an answer, as the Pope.
>                   Tell him this tale; and from the mouth of
>                       England
>                   Add this much more,—that no Italian priest
>                   Shall tithe or toll in our dominions:
>                   But as we, under heaven, are supreme head,
>                   So, under Him that great supremacy,
>                   Where we do reign, we will alone uphold,
>                   Without the assistance of a mortal hand.
>                   So tell the Pope, all reverence set apart
>                   To him and his usurp'd authority.
> *King Philip.* Brother of England, you blaspheme in this.
> *King John.* Though you and all the kings of Christendom
>                   Are led so grossly by this meddling priest,
>                   Dreading the curse that money may buy out,
>                   And by the merit of vile gold, dross, dust,
>                   Purchase corrupted pardon of a man,
>                   Who in that sale sells pardon from himself,
>                   Though you and all the rest so grossly led,
>                   This juggling witchcraft with revenue cherish,
>                   Yet I alone, alone do me oppose
>                   Against the Pope, and count his friends my foes.
> *Pandulph.* Then, by the lawful power that I have,
>                   Thou shalt stand curs'd and excommunicate:
>                   And blessed shall he be that doth revolt
>                   From his allegiance to an heretic;
>                   And meritorious shall that hand be call'd,
>                   Canonized and worshipp'd as a saint,
>                   That takes away by any secret course
>                   Thy hateful life.[11]

[11] *King John,* Act III, Scene I, lines 135-178.

In looking at this passage and these speeches we must remember that the King John who calls the Pope "unworthy," is without a doubt the villain of Shakespeare's play.[12] Then we must remember that the "anointed deputies of heaven," the anointed kings by divine right, were in an actual physical sense anointed at coronation by a churchman. The priest was to John a meddling priest and the pope's authority usurped authority only in relation to England and English affairs—and it was again a question of politics and not of religion.

Shakespeare was writing with his theme clearly in mind and could not paint John any whiter than he was when he opposed the Church, though he did paint him blacker than he was when he maltreated young Arthur. It was a political crisis and clearly so and Shakespeare is careful to emphasize this political character. He did not make John a hero, and he likewise came far from making him a doctrinal Protestant. He changed the old play to leave out the religious element and to show the struggle as it was. It was a political conflict in which religion unfortunately was slightly confused, if not through a plurality of causes, at least through a combination of elements.

The alteration of history, the insertion of speeches which were never spoken, the invention of incidents,[13] and real historical anachronisms, not merely detailed ones like the clock of ancient Rome[14] and the unfounded University of Witten-

[12] His compelled granting of Magna Charta is even neglected—one of the greatest and most beneficial gains of his or any other reign—as is also the pope's forbidding of its observance.
[13] Cf. *Richard II*, Act II, Scene III, lines 99-100.
[14] *Julius Caesar*.

berg,[15] but actual changes in the unity and order of events[16] —these things in error are forgotten when Shakespeare is read as a whole and is found to have written with a noteworthy fidelity to the main temper of the circumstances, to have given us a true impression if not a true chronicle.

## II

History like the drama is developed from the conflict of opposing forces. It is our loss, therefore, that Shakespeare skips over more than a hundred and sixty years after the death of John. He has given us no picture of the reign of Henry III (1216–1272) and his religious troubles, he who "would have been a good priest but was a bad king"; no picture of Edward I (1272–1307), one of the best of the Catholic kings who clashed with the papacy, who really established Parliament and placed nationalism over feudalism; no picture of Edward II (1307–1327), "a hollow counterfeit of his father," whose fall inspired Marlowe and renders that dramatist's works more memorable; no picture of Edward III (1327–1377), during whose reign the popes at Avignon were opposed for diplomatic rather than unfaithful reasons, and "Old John of Gaunt" had allied himself with Wiclif for ecclesiastical reform and pretended to an anticlerical popularity. But if there does exist this great gap between Shakespeare and history through the thirteenth and fourteenth centuries, the plays of *Richard II*, the two

[15] *Hamlet*.
[16] *King John* is one good example of this carelessness about dates; *Henry VIII* is another.

parts of *Henry IV*, *Henry V*, the three parts of *Henry VI*, and the story of *Richard III* make up for the earlier deficiencies.[17]

Here we find open before us "the purple testament of bleeding war." There was civil war and there was war with France. Shakespeare has told of the contenders struggling for the crown, of usurpers mounting the throne itself and there facing down upon the anointed king, of attempts to "wipe off the dust that hides our sceptre's gilt," of what the ancient chronicler Hall named "the unquiete tyme of Kyng Henry the Fourth," of the tragic enormity and fierce complexions in the age when Richard, Duke of Gloster, plotted and murdered for his unwarranted ends.

It seems as if Shakespeare almost aimed to avoid religious questions. He begins the play of *Richard II* in 1398, recounting only the fall of that monarch and telling nothing of Wat Tyler's rebellion, the Peasants' Revolt of 1381, Wiclif and the Lollards, nor of John Ball, "the clerical demagogue."[18] In the Epilogue to the second part of *Henry IV* he identifies his famous character, Sir John Falstaff, with Lord Cobham, saying "Oldcastle died a [Lollard] martyr and this is not he," to which Dowden commentates: "Shakespeare changed the name because he did not wish wantonly to offend the Protestant party nor gratify the Roman Catholics." He carefully avoids the religious implications and possibilities in the character of Henry V, which many men have been fain to find there, and which many others have

---

[17] Though there is an apparent break between the years 1461–1483, there really is none; Shakespeare tells the story of Edward IV and Edward V continuously, though chronologically compressed, in the plays which precede and follow.

[18] The quotation is from Goldwin Smith.

even read into Shakespeare.[19] Churchmen appear, to be sure, in connection with Church affairs as when Cardinal Bouchier protests to Buckingham against a plan to "infringe the holy privilege of blessed sanctuary,"[20] as when the Bishop of Ely is carefully avoided while Gloster plots for advancement,[21] when a clerical "tutor" and a priest "Sir John" appear for a moment and then leave,[22] and when the Bishop of Ely and the Archbishop of Canterbury worry among themselves about Church lands.[23] And Church paraphernalia and ritual come in from time to time, as the religious background of the age required. To be faithful in the picture one must put these things in; to leave them out would be holding an untrue mirror up to nature. Richard II gets Norfolk and Bolingbroke to take an oath on the hilt of a sword which forms a cross;[24] Henry V is insistent on the final rites of the Church for a departed soul;[25] Richard II tells the queen to cloister herself "in some religious house,"[26] and later thinks of following the same course himself:

> I'll give my jewels for a set of beads,
> My gorgeous palace for a hermitage,
> My gay apparel for an alms-man's gown,
> My figur'd goblets for a dish of wood,
> My sceptre for a palmer's walking staff,

---

[19] Cf. the *Shakespearean Commentaries* of Dr. G. G. Gervinus, translated by F. E. Bunnet, revised ed. (London, 1875), pp. 340 ff.
[20] *III Henry VI*, Act III, Scene I, lines 37-43.
[21] *III Henry VI*, Act III, Scene IV.
[22] *III Henry VI*, Act I, Scene III, and Act III, Scene II.
[23] *Henry V*, Act I, Scene I.
[24] The same appears in *Hamlet*, Act I, Scene V, line 160.
[25] *Henry V*, Act IV, Scene VIII, line 121.
[26] *Richard II*, Act V, Scene I, line 23.

> My subjects for a pair of carved saints,
> And my large kingdom for a little grave.

There are proper and dignified references to rosary beads, in *Richard II*, and in the second part of *Henry VI;* Bardolph, very follower of Henry's very intimate Falstaff, was executed for robbing a church.[27] Nor should we forget the tribute to banish'd Norfolk's fine crusading spirit, who

>                                 fought
> For Jesu Christ in glorious Christian field,
> Streaming the ensign of the Christian cross
> Against black pagans, Turks, and Saracens:
> And toil'd with works of war, retir'd himself
> To Italy; and there, at Venice, gave
> His body to that pleasant country's earth,
> And his pure soul unto his captain Christ,
> Under whose colors he had fought so long.[28]

The last lines of *Richard II* express a wish in the heart of Henry IV to go likewise to the Holy Land as penance for his faults, and this idea appears and reappears at intervals as a serious but deferred intent in both parts of *Henry IV*.

But no amount of imagination can make plausible an attempt to interpret these years, when there was really so much done in the way of religious invective and anticlerical protest, as of prime ecclesiastical importance. That Shakespeare had imagination is not to be denied; but he wisely did not make such a foolish attempt. He emphasized in these hundred years the political struggle between rivals for

---

[27] *Henry V*, Act III, Scene VI.
[28] *Richard II*, Act IV, Scene I, lines 91-100.

the title of English King; and such churchmen as enter in, are represented only in the character of politicians.[29] That he failed to dwell on the very important steps toward the development of Parliament was possibly due to the fact that it would not please Tudor royalty and partly because it might even fail to interest a populace who lived under the Tudor "strong monarchy." But these churchmen who dabbled in politics did interest, because both the royal family and the groundlings knew the type well. The principal ecclesiastics turning their minds to such things were four.

The Bishop of Carlisle in *Richard II* is painted as "a clergyman of noble reverence," who urges Richard to warlike ways and later, defending him against calumniators, predicts the dire internecine strife to follow.[30]

The Abbot of Westminster in the same play is "the grand conspirator" who plots for the reinstatement of Richard and has the rebellious heads actually meet at his house in Westminster.[31]

The Archbishop of York who appears in *I Henry IV* and is executed in *II Henry IV*, acts for mere revenge of his brother Scrope's death, excites and leads and plans and schemes and even portions off England for the rising Percies.

[29] In three particulars Shakespeare has departed from history: (1) There is no warrant for the speech assigned to Chicheley in *Henry V*, urging the King to war; (2) no authority for having intriguing Richard III and Buckingham get theatrical support from two bishops and a prayer book to impress the Mayor of London; (3) and he did not make the Bishop Arundel in *II Henry IV* protest against the execution of Scrope, as he legitimately might have done.

[30] *Richard II*, Act III, Scene III, lines 178-185; and Act IV, Scene I, lines 113-149.

[31] *Richard II*, Act IV, Scene I, lines 326-333; Act V, Scene II; and Act V, Scene VI, line 19.

Scrope and his clerical confederates may have been exasperated by the heavy draughts the King had made on clerical revenues; they may have believed his government to be secretly inclined to the confiscation of church property; or the archbishop, a political and military prelate, may simply have shared the mutinous and intriguing spirit of the oligarchy.[32]

He, it was, probably who drew up the "things articulate," and turning insurrection to religion, had them

> Proclaim'd at market-crosses, read in churches,
> To face the garment of rebellion
> With some fine color that may please the eye.[33]

The subsequent troubles with the pope resulting from Henry IV's summary dealing with an ecclesiastic are glossed over by Shakespeare:

> Scrope was taken in armed, unprovoked, and criminal rebellion. Whatever might be his avowed aims, there could be no doubt that he and his party, if successful, would have dethroned the King. . . . The country was not to be devastated and dismembered with impunity by political intriguers styling themselves apostles of the religion of Christ.[34]

Shakespeare seems to have treated him in the history plays as he deserved, as a factious rebel and a politician rather than as a churchman.

[32] Goldwin Smith, *The United Kingdom*, Vol. I, page 246.
[33] Cf. *I Henry IV*, Act V, Scene I; *II Henry IV*, Act I, Scene III; Act IV, Scenes I and II.
[34] Goldwin Smith, *The United Kingdom*, Vol. I, pp. 247-8.

Cardinal Beaufort, because of the heated conversational clashes with Gloster, comes in for so much vituperation, though it was at the hands of one of Shakespeare's most renowned villains, that Goldwin Smith has called him "sublimely slandered."[35] He is deprecated as a "politician," as a "presumptuous priest," a "proud prelate," an "ambitious churchman," as "impious Beaufort, that false priest"; said to be "more haughty than the devil," a "haughty cardinal, more like a soldier than a man o' the Church," who never in the year goes to church except to pray against his enemies.[36] He is painted as a very active cardinal, though cursed at by Gloster and curtly told by the King to practise his own preachings; he hires spies, indulges in undignified squabbles, urges the King against Gloster, conspires his fall, and registers an objection to church extortions made by Suffolk. This last, the objection, is the only act which pertains to his position as a churchman, so completely has Shakespeare deleted the religious element from his historical play.

These men, the four of them, are politicians who also chance to wear the cloth. It is true, of course, that they imperil the dignity of their Church by engaging in the game of dynastic intrigue, and the question then arises if, at the fall of each, they conduct themselves as politicians or as churchmen. The Abbot of Westminster "yielded up his body to the grave . . . with clog of conscience and sour melancholy," and Beaufort died "blaspheming God and cursing men on earth"—these two at least were sketched by Shakespeare. And well might they have exclaimed with Wolsey,

[35] Goldwin Smith, *The United Kingdom*, Vol. I, p. 264.
[36] *I Henry VI*, Act I, Scene I, Scene III; Act III, Scene I; Act V, Scene II, Scene IV; *II Henry VI*, Act I, Scene I; Act II, Scene I.

> Had I but serv'd my God with half the zeal
> I serv'd my king, He would not in mine age
> Have left me naked to mine enemies.

Which leads us to a double point on which the conclusion of this essay will turn, the ambitious activities of these churchmen and the character of Wolsey in exciting years for the English Church.

### III

The play of *Henry VIII*, as we have it now, is a poor dramatic representation of one of the most dramatic moments of history. To Shakespearean enthusiasts it is some consolation that more than two thirds of this piece was done by Fletcher and not by the Warwickshire Will.[37] Our poet did not, in this his last play, tell "very frankly of how England was torn from the Church by a brutal king to satisfy his lust."[38] There is a possibility that he projected a drama on the final separation as the one great historical event of the reign, and that a few scenes already written toward that end were focused about the fall of Wolsey and scattered through the play by Fletcher, who acted either as collaborator or as adapter. At any rate, Shakespeare avoided the issue, a tremendous climax of interest for any poet. He makes no reference to the Act of Supremacy, or to the dissolution of the monasteries, and only a scant statement concerning Sir Thomas More. The actual facts

---

[37] The introduction to the play in the Tudor Shakespeare indicates the exact scenes—showing that the most noted pieces of declamation are from the hand of Fletcher.

[38] As James J. Walsh says in the *Catholic World*, April, 1916, p. 42.

of the dissolution would have made a powerful resolution of the dramatic theme.

> Rapine was not statesmanship, nor did it walk in statesmanlike ways. The hour of the monasteries had come, but dissolution might have been gradual. It might have respected local circumstance and feeling. In the wild and ill-peopled north monasteries were still useful as hospices, as almshouses, as dispensaries, as record offices, as schools, perhaps in a rough way as centres of civilization. Their faith was still that of the people; their prayers and Masses for the dead were still prized. Their destruction and the religious innovations of the government brought on a dangerous insurrection in the north, called the Pilgrimage of Grace,[39] in the suppression of which the government showed its perfidy as well as its savage recklessness of blood.[40]

These destructions were bad enough, but not so bad as the uselessness of most of the purposes to which the seized properties were converted.[41]

> Some was spent in national defences, a small part in the foundation of new bishoprics. Far the greater part became the prey of the King and his minions. The vast estates of noble houses remain monuments to the confiscation, and they bound those houses to the cause of Protestantism and a Protestant government so long as the conflict lasted. This is the origin, and hence were derived the politics, of the houses of Russell, Cavendish, Seymour, Grey, Dudley, Sidney, Cecil,

---

[39] H. de B. Gibbins: *Industry in England*, pp. 203-4, assigns other causes for this, notably the extensive enclosures.
[40] Goldwin Smith, *The United Kingdom*, Vol. I, pp. 335-6.
[41] H. de B. Gibbins, *Industry in England*, p. 203.

Herbert, Fitzwilliam. Rich, which replaced the feudal baronage of the Middle Ages, linked to Protestantism and constitutionalism by their possession of Church lands.[42]

Thus fully has the characteristic temper of this great tendency been sketched simply to indicate what Shakespeare avoided in his play. The financial element was a strong motive in the mind of that Henry who had been so prodigal with his nation's money; it was undoubtedly an underlying cause and incentive. Mr. Goldwin Smith, a political historian, has said, "The sole cause of Henry's secession from the papacy and of religious revolution so far as he personally was concerned was his desire for a divorce."[43] And it is not exaggerating to say that where Henry was concerned, personal causes were liable to be immediate causes. Thus this play which is called Shakespeare's, though it does not deal with the real essential center of the reign of Henry VIII, does represent some of the important facts leading toward that center.

The play is the play of Wolsey, the cunning, ambitious Cardinal of York, pitted against a simple woman far from her home and friends, and afterward pitted against the "strong monarch," Henry VIII himself. As Katharine is made to say, "all hoods make not monks"; and in the case of Wolsey, "cardinal sins and hollow hearts"[44] go about in churchmen's robes. Wolsey is a scheming politician, not a true representative of his Church:

[42] Goldwin Smith, *The United Kingdom*, Vol. I, p. 334. See also H. Belloc, *The Historic Thames* (Wayfarer's Library Edition), pp. 127-8, 140.
[43] Goldwin Smith, *The United Kingdom*, Vol. I, p. 318.
[44] *Henry VIII*, Act III, Scene I, lines 23, 104.

> No man's pie is freed,
> From his ambitious finger.⁴⁵

> His thinkings are below the moon not worth
> His serious considering.⁴⁶

He is desirous of sitting in the papal chair; he falsely denies true charges of heavy and extortionate taxations; he maintains a rich house in unnecessary luxury;⁴⁷ by his manipulations and attempted interference he brought Henry to condemn the "dilatory sloth and tricks of Rome."⁴⁸ To be sure, we find him condemning Sir Thomas Bullen as "a spleeny Lutheran," and Cranmer as "an heretic, an arch-one," and magnanimously praising his successor, Sir Thomas More, as "a learned man" who will "do justice for truth's sake and his conscience." When his overthrow is complete and he pauses to say "a long farewell" to all his greatness, he then turns to thoughts of God. Not as the Abbot of Westminster or Cardinal Beaufort did Wolsey die; but, in the calm and serenity of a great man, "he died fearing God." Yet there is little doubt that he ceased to worship Ambition and began to think of God only when he fell,

> like Lucifer
> Never to hope again.

It is a late repentance.

⁴⁵ *Henry VIII*, Act I, Scene I, lines 52-53.
⁴⁶ *Henry VIII*, Act III, Scene II, lines 134-135.
⁴⁷ One of the points charged against him was that he changed the rushes on his floors every day—an extravagant waste.
⁴⁸ *Henry VIII*, Act II, Scene IV, line 237.

> I have ventured,
> Like little wanton boys that swim on bladders,
> This many summers in a sea of glory
> But far beyond my depth. My high-blown pride
> At length broke under me, and now has left me,
> Weary and old with service, to the mercy
> Of a rude stream, that must forever hide me.
> Vain pomp and glory of this world, I hate ye!
> I feel my heart new open'd.

The fact that Fletcher wrote most of the phrases we have quoted here,[49] and not Shakespeare, is beside the point. "Love and meekness become a churchman better than ambition." This is a play of ambition and not of religion. Its central point is the fall of Wolsey and not the conflict of the Churches. Though it hinges about the divorce, the excommunication by the pope—sweeping across Europe to strike at the crown of Henry—is not brought forward. There is no clear clash between a king and a foreign papacy, as in *King John*. The old tragic idea of the fall of princes here comes back again, the execution of Buckingham, the injustice done to Katharine, and the reduction of Wolsey. These fell indeed. And their fall was the same. Politics contrived with politics and religion was only accidental.

### IV

Thus we have a similarity in treatment in *King John* and in *Henry VIII*. Nor does the tendency end there. It extends as well to the plays which cover the years between. Shake-

---

[49] Also the final passages about Elizabeth: "In her days God shall be truly known."

speare has followed the same method continuously, a method of detachment. He has detached himself from the theses of both parties. History and historical drama march on parallel paths to the same end. We are in the field of political endeavor where politicians happened also to be abbots, bishops, and cardinals. Shakespeare recorded the facts as historical facts, presenting them in the dramatic mood as well as in the dramatic manner. But if he did not alter the personalities of prelates who held state offices, he likewise did not take advantage of their religious connections to assail them unduly. He was fair, remarkably so, and held no brief for either party. The Elizabethan age was a time of religious controversy and the temptation must have been great to take sides with one faction or another and so gain cheap and calculated applause.[50] We have seen how the particular dignitaries were handled. We have observed how the chief emphasis was a political emphasis. The art and mind of Shakespeare were bent toward ecclesiastical dissension. So, naturally, he proceeded—though not so dispassionately —at least almost as impartially as history. He discounted biased feeling in the clerical chronicles from which he drew and discounted the prejudices of the "good Queen Bess." It was a middle course. He steered it fairly and well.

We shall next turn from these historical plays to those which, dependent upon invention, may be classed as fiction.

[50] Joan of Arc only is severely handled. He upholds her in the early scenes, but treats her harshly after her fall. *I Henry VI*, Act V, Scenes III and IV.

# 7

## Clerical Characters in Shakespeare

COLERIDGE has declared that "the transitional link between the epic poem and the drama is the historical drama." Shakespeare translated the formless type of the early chronicle play into a powerful Marlowesque *Richard III* and an exalted and heroic *Henry V*. Then when he had broken free from epic chronology, when he had mastered the historical drama until in his hands its epic qualities were lost and its dramatic appeal was predominant, he passed out of this field and in the full strength of his maturity produced such works as *Hamlet, Lear,* and *Macbeth,* whose appeal shall never die.

It might be possible to divide the works of Shakespeare into three groups: (*a*) the historical plays, (*b*) the dramas which pretend only to fiction, (*c*) those which might be entitled *historical fiction*. This third group, represented for example by *Macbeth, Julius Caesar,* and *Lear,* consists of plots which, however much they owed to Plutarch or Holinshed, are so transfigured by the genius who prepared them for the stage that sources are forgotten and the dramatist is remembered. So great liberties did Shakespeare take with the materials handed down to him and so magnificently did he employ his art that these cannot be called chronicle plays, ought not to be considered as betwixt and between, but must be ranked as works where a master genius gives imagination full play. They are no more dependent upon original sources than *The Winter's Tale* is upon Robert Greene, or *Measure for Measure* upon the Italian Cinthio. It has seemed desirable therefore to put all these remaining dramas, which were not among the ten history plays discussed in our previous chapter, into a single large final group whose chief source was, by and large, in the imaginative mind of Shakespeare.

He lived in the expanding age of Elizabeth, a time of change and growth in matters material and spiritual. The explorers and the Merchant Adventurers were sailing far with an almost lyric enthusiasm, over oceans on whose water was even then being written the dramatic epic of British Empire. Poets, philosophers, and playwrights sought pastures new and seas as yet uncharted. It was the time of adventure and of travel. No mere verbal bombast but a real yearning to know the unknown and to accomplish the impossible drew these men forth, as already quoted:

> Some, to the wars, to try their fortunes there;
> Some, to discover islands far away;
> Some, to the studious universities.

This was the spirit which sent Valentine

> To see the wonders of the world abroad,[1]

and put on the lips of Benedict the lines which to us seem boastful but in those days were usual.

[1] *Two Gentlemen of Verona*, Act I, Scene I.

Will your grace command me any service to the world's end? I will go on the slightest errand now to the Antipodes that you can devise to send me on; I will fetch you a toothpicker now from the furthest inch of Asia, bring you the length of Prester John's foot, fetch you a hair off the great Cham's beard, do you any embassage to the Pigmies.[2]

They believed that "home-keeping youths have ever homely wits" and when their fervent imaginations wandered into the great places of the spirit, the cargo they brought home again was as rich and inspiring as the ivory of Africa, the gold of India, the silks of Cipango, and the perfumes of Arabia. It was a boundless age, boundless in thought, word, and deed.

In the face of such vastness some apology must be made for conducting a detailed study of some one phase of such greatness. That is the method of all scholarship. The dilettante is sometimes interesting but rarely sound. The specialist like Professor Wallace spends many years among the legal documents of the Public Record Office and at last discovers a hidden fact which may make a world of difference. Another careful scholar finds a contemporary allusion tucked into an odd line and so gives a new basis for determining the date of a given play. Another reads a forgotten book and indicates a hitherto unknown source for one of the plots. Thus it goes, and an army of gentle scholars write many volumes to elucidate a few plays, but in the end their combined labors have given a new insight and added a new touch to a rough painting, slowly and carefully transforming an outline sketch into a full portrait. A. Mézières[3] has studied the historical dramas parting the

[2] *Much Ado about Nothing*, Act II, Scene I.
[3] *Shakespeare, ses œuvres et ses critiques.*

characters into groups—the women, the children, the people, the lords, the prelates, the kings. So any specialist is justified in expressing his opinions on his special part of Shakespeare, provided always he is well acquainted with the other broad facts and is not intolerant toward the generalizations of other specialists on their special points. For instance, no one quarrels with William Burgess[4] for commenting on the Biblical characters in Shakespeare, but all sane men must quarrel with him for attempting a religious interpretation and exaltation of the sonnets which Sir Sidney Lee has shown to be amorous convention and literature.

So when we come to write of certain religious elements in his works we must bear in mind the lesson of *The Merchant of Venice*, that prejudice based on religious reasons is usually unreasonable. We should not quarrel but should do our work of scrutiny and formulate our judgments with the greatest detachment possible. We would not have men smile at our scholars and remark, in the words of Vergil,

> tantaene animis coelestibus irae.

One thing at least is certain, though the rest may not all be lies. As Charles Cowden Clarke so justly said, "He has, in short, never fostered the wicked, or pandered to the Pharisee and self-worshipper; his all abounding charity is in itself a rebuke to the 'too-seeming holy,' who *talk* of grace, yet shut the gates of mercy upon the weak and the frail." It was far from his purpose, as from ours, to change dramatic conflict into religious quarrel.

[4] *The Bible in Shakespeare*, New York, 1903.

I

One of Shakespeare's earliest plays, *The Two Gentlemen of Verona*, with its scene laid in Catholic Italy, comes within the field of our investigation on account of the religious paraphernalia continually introduced, and four plays of what is called his "third period," *Hamlet, Romeo and Juliet, Measure for Measure,* and *Much Ado About Nothing*, the first for many reasons, the others on account of the prominence given to monastic characters whom he has hailed forth from their cloisters to bring "a man of comfort" onto the distressed stage. Of these monks from the various undesignated orders, Schlegel has said: "It is deserving of remark, that Shakespeare, amidst the rancor of religious parties, takes a delight in painting the condition of a monk, and always represents his influence as beneficial. We find in him none of the black and knavish monks, which an enthusiasm for Protestantism, rather than poetical inspiration, has suggested to some of our modern poets. Shakespeare merely gives his monks an inclination to busy themselves in the affairs of others, after renouncing the world for themselves. . . . Such are the parts acted by the monk in *Romeo and Juliet*, and another in *Much Ado About Nothing*, and even by the duke,[5] whom, contrary to the well-known proverb, the cowl really seems to make a monk."

When Shakespeare wrote, it was many years since the dissolution of the monasteries and the break with Rome; but, as every reader of *Come Rack! Come Rope!* knows, there were many Catholics and much Catholic sentiment in England at the time. We are not surprised, then, to find things and facts pertinent to the Catholic religion in his

[5] In *Measure for Measure*.

plays. "The boyhood of Shakespeare was passed in a country town where the practices of the Catholic Church had not been wholly eradicated." His mother lived and died a Catholic. His father was summoned as a recusant for not attending the Sunday services of the Anglicans. Warwickshire was distinctly out of sympathy with the new establishment of Edward and Elizabeth. Heine has pointed out that it was not till later that the Puritans succeeded in plucking away flower by flower, and utterly rooting up the religion of the past, that popular faith of the Middle Ages which yet existed with all its magic in men's hearts, and held its own in manners, customs, and views.

In the plays of Shakespeare we have passing notices of these. "Porteus, in the first scene,[6] says,

> I will be thy beadsman, Valentine.

Shakespeare had, doubtless, seen the rosary still worn, and the 'beads bidden,' perhaps even in his own house. Julia compares the strength of her affection to the unwearied steps of 'the true-devoted pilgrim.'[7] Shakespeare had, per-

---

[6] *The Two Gentlemen of Verona*, Act I, Scene I.

[7] Act II, Scene VII. Knight says: "The comparison which Julia makes between the ardor of her passion and the enthusiasm of the pilgrim is exceedingly beautiful. When travelling was a business of considerable danger and personal suffering, the pilgrim who was not weary 'to traverse kingdoms with his feeble steps,' to encounter the perils of a journey to Rome, or Loreto, or Compostella, or Jerusalem, was a person to be looked upon as thoroughly in earnest. In the time of Shakespeare the pilgrimages to the tomb of St. Thomas à Becket, at Canterbury, which Chaucer has rendered immortal, were discontinued; and few, perhaps, undertook the sea voyage to Jerusalem. But the pilgrimage to the shrine of St. James, or St. Jago, the patron saint of Spain, at Compostella, was undertaken by all classes of Catholics. The House of Our Lady at Loreto was, however, the great object of the devotee's vows; and, at particular seasons, there were not fewer than two hundred thousand pilgrims visiting it at once."

haps, heard the tale of some ancient denizen of a ruined abbey who had made the pilgrimage to the shrine of Our Lady of Loretto, or had even visited the sacred tomb at Jerusalem. Thurio and Porteus are to meet at 'St. Gregory's well.' This is the only instance in Shakespeare in which a holy well is mentioned; but how often must he have seen the country people, in the early summer morning or after their daily labor, resorting to the fountain which had been hallowed from the Saxon times as under the guardian influence of some venerated saint!"[8] The Sacrament of Penance is mentioned as well as the idea behind it.

> Who by repentance is not satisfied
> Is nor of heaven nor earth.[9]

A confessor is provided for condemned Claudio in *Measure for Measure*. Silvia and Juliet are alike in that each elope when going to usual confession.[10]

Why exactly it was necessary to introduce into the plot of the *Menæchini* of Plautus or the *Didymi* of Menander, with the scene Asia Minor and the audience Londonese, the priory in the last act of the *Comedy of Errors*, why Antipholus of Syracuse can run nowhere else but to sanctuary, why the quiet firmness and calm of the Lady Abbess was essential to the resolution of the plot—why all these points of dramatic construction were absolutely necessary it is not ours to know. Suffice the facts to record more Catholic elements in Shakespearean drama. Many times in the plays

[8] From Knight's *Pictorial Shakespeare*.
[9] *Two Gentlemen of Verona*, Act V, Scene IV.
[10] *Measure for Measure*, Act II, Scene I; *Two Gentlemen of Verona*, Act IV, Scene III; *Romeo and Juliet*, Act II, Scene VI.

## Clerical Characters in Shakespeare 125

there are references to these matters, chance allusions which would certainly never have been introduced by a fervent Protestant or by a playwright who thought his audience fervently Protestant. Here follows a partial list of those not already mentioned, that we may pass on to broader matters of interpretation and imagination:

> Friar Lawrence . . .
> . . . in penance wand'ring through the forest.
> (*Two Gentlemen of Verona*—V, ii.)
> We'll have flesh for holidays, fish for fasting-days.
> (*Pericles*—II, i.)
> His kissing is as full of sanctity as the touch of holy bread.
> (*As You Like It*—III, iv.)
> St. Nicholas, be thy speed [the patron saint of scholars and clerks]. (*Two Gentlemen of Verona*—III, i.)
> Have you prayed tonight, Desdemona? . . .
> I would not kill thy unprepared spirit.
> (*Othello*—V, ii.)
> He should the bearers put to sudden death,
> Not shriving-time allow'd. (*Hamlet*—V, ii.)
> There is a monastery two miles off.
> (*Merchant of Venice*—III, iv.)
> She [Portia] doth stray about
> By holy crosses, where she kneels and prays.
> (*Merchant of Venice*—V, i.)
> Good morrow, father.
> Benedicite!
> (*Romeo and Juliet*—II, iii.)
> O, for my beads! I cross me for a sinner.
> (*Comedy of Errors*—II, ii.)

The most noteworthy characteristic about these allusions

is the fact that they are all unnecessary. No principle of dramaturgy demands these words, and yet they are there. No convention or tendency of contemporary stagecraft would give warrant for them as usual theatrical figures or phrases. Shakespeare's rustic characters used mostly the conventional dialect of stage rustics, the southwestern forms, not those current in the poet's native Warwickshire, yet there is no similar thing to be said of his religious characterizations or pious language. Shakespeare was simply trying hard to give a true Italian flavor to the narrative wine he was putting into British dramatic bottles. Yet in none of his plays where the scene is in Milan, Verona, or Messina, does he catch the very spirit of the country so well as in *The Merchant of Venice*, where the religious trappings of a formal, and hints of a subtle, nature are least in evidence. So that it may be possible to venture that these elements were inserted, not to gain local Italian color, but simply, in an almost unconscious and unnecessary way. This would mean more. It would mean that Shakespeare was drawing on his native Warwickshire for little exclamations and sentences, reminiscent of things he had known about him as well as he knew that bank where the wild thyme grows.

There are two or three minor prelates, curates, or what not, which demand our attention for a moment or so. They are all of English stock and spring of English tradition, without attempt at localization in conformity with the narrative. Sir Nathaniel, "the very quintessence of conceit and complacency," in *Love's Labours Lost*, is presumably attached to the court of Ferdinand of Navarre. Sir Hugh Evans, the peppery Welsh parson copied after Fluellen, is a contemporary of Falstaff and therefore of Henry V. But there is nothing Catholic about them. Sir Nathaniel is obviously a satire on the spouting young churchmen of Elizabeth's day, and Sir Hugh comes posthaste out of Windsor with those merry wives, Mistress Page and Mistress Ford, too fresh and flippant to have traveled across even a half a century. It is not possible to push the chronology too hard and to claim them as Catholics, better let them remain as anachronisms. And very amusing anachronisms they are, created for the sake of humor. Sir Hugh leads in pinching Falstaff at the revels round Herne's oak to make him roar, and Sir Nathaniel by his fantastic display of doltish erudition makes his hearers roar—with laughter.

Nor are these Anglican curates, or the representations of them, the only religious persons handled ungently by the pen of Shakespeare. Petruchio starts to sing:

> It was the friar of orders grey,
> As he walked on his way—[11]

and no one knows what his loose tongue might have uttered, had the chance rogue not pulled awry in plucking off his master's boots and interrupted the song. Not even the version in Percy's *Reliques* can tell us, for Petruchio was by repute an unconventional and irresponsible and irreverent chap. His conduct at the marriage is enough to stop us from indiscreetly inquiring too much:

> When the priest
> Should ask, if Katherine should be his wife,

[11] *The Taming of the Shrew*, Act IV, Scene I.

> "Aye, by gogs-wouns," quoth he, and swore so loud,
> That, all amaz'd, the priest let fall the book;
> And, as he stoop'd again to take it up,
> The mad-brain'd bridegroom took him such a cuff
> That down fell priest and book, and book and priest.[12]

Yet though this can be said to be written entirely in character, to bring out the extreme activity of Petruchio in his attempts to tame the shrew, the same cannot be said of the following:

> I know thou art religious
> And hast a thing within thee called conscience,
> With twenty popish tricks and ceremonies
> Which I have seen thee careful to observe,
> Therefore I urge thy oath; for that I know
> An idiot holds his bauble for a god
> And keeps the oath which by that god he swears,
> To that I'll urge him.[13]

This is the worst thing that is found in any of the plays of Shakespeare. In the historical dramas only is the pope mentioned and then legitimately only, where history demands it. In no place other than in this anachronistic spot in a Roman play is there a lapse into the slurring Briticism, "popish tricks." But it so happens that this play of *Titus Andronicus* is one in which the question of disputed authorship is most engaged. Peele, Greene, Kyd, or Lodge may have written that phrase "popish tricks," a scurrility to which Shakespeare nowhere else stooped. Thus, if it can-

---

[12] *The Taming of the Shrew*, Act III, Scene II.
[13] *Titus Andronicus*, Act V, Scene I.

# Clerical Characters in Shakespeare

not definitely be said that Shakespeare did not say this thing, it also cannot definitely be charged against him even though the speaker, Aaron, elsewhere shows the marks of a Shakespearean manner.

II

We now leave behind all the passages which might be uncomplimentary and pass on to the particular religious in the particular plays.

In *As You Like It* we find the colorless Sir Oliver Martext with his chapel in the forest[14] ready to perform the matrimonial rites, although at the end it is Hymen who joins all the marriages. Yet Olympian theology and Greek mythology finally give way to Christianity, for the happy consummation of the plot is brought about by "an old religious man" who converts Duke Frederick from his usurped throne to a life of piety.[15]

Again, in *Twelfth Night*, it is the same Sacrament of Marriage which brings a priest on the stage with Olivia to unite her with Sebastian,[16] and, though he has no lines at all on his first entrance, when he appears again to tell of what transpired "underneath that consecrated roof" of his chantry, the priest describes a marriage as worthy as it was pure:

> A contract of eternal bond of love,
> Confirm'd by mutual joinder of your hands,
> Attested by the holy close of lips,

[14] Act III, Scene III.
[15] Act V, Scene IV.
[16] Act IV, Scene III.

> Strengthen'd by interchangement of your rings,
> And all the ceremony of this compact
> Seal'd in my function, by my testimony.[17]

In *Much Ado About Nothing* we have another of the famous friars of Shakespeare doing good to the world and interfering in worldly affairs to relieve the harshness of unjust circumstances. When slander interrupts the wedding ceremony of Claudio and Hero with a fabricated "tale of guilt," the Friar Francis remains silent. He is at the ceremony, as he is at the double marriage performed at the close of the play, in an official and not in a personal capacity, to represent the Church and the Church only, not himself. In this respect he does not differ from other clerical characters in these plays. They perform the offices of the Church at the grave or at the marriage altar; they do their duty as it is clearly defined for them, fulfilling the dramatic need which brought the cloth upon the stage. But this does not satisfy Friar Francis. After the shameful disruption upon which the plot hinges and by which the needed suspense is gained, Friar Francis's first words are:

> Have comfort, lady!

His first duty is to console. His next is to dispose and order things aright. He suggests the solution of the trouble and expresses a firm belief in Hero's innocence. There is much humanity and keen psychological insight in a priest. He seems to have no real facts on which to base his opinion, yet Friar Francis is right. Perhaps he is right because he,

[17] Act V, Scene I.

like Chesterton's "Father Brown," grasps the essentials in moral evidence. "I go by a man's eyes and voice, and by what subjects he chooses—and avoids. I attach a good deal of importance to vague ideas. All these things that 'aren't evidence' are what convince me. I think a moral impossibility the biggest of all impossibilities." And probably the "moral impossibility" of Hero's guilt was what urged her innocence in the eyes of the Friar who had heard her confessions since childhood. At any rate, he had the pleasure of retiring again into his role as officer of the Church and of celebrating her marriage.

In *Measure for Measure*, there are two more friars, Thomas and Peter, of whom Peter is silent, but Thomas has to his credit a splendid and sensible criticism addressed to the Duke Vincentio against sudden and unjust rigor in enforcing an old law which might be said to have lapsed with the passing of time. But the chief monk in this play is not a monk at all. As we have said above, the Duke Vincentio disproves the fact that the cowl does not make the monk. He acts the part naturally, even to deception, and rivals Friar Lawrence and Friar Francis of the two more famous plays by the way he conducts himself in the interviews with Juliet and with Claudio, though in the last act just before the disclosure,[18] he seems in his arrogance once more the Duke and less the monk.

But the most appealing figure in this comedy, *Measure for Measure*, is Isabella, the novice of St. Clare in those humble robes in which Schlegel found her "a very angel of light." Shakespeare did not stint himself in her favor, "a thing enskied and sainted, an immortal spirit." Furnivall

---

[18] Act II, Scene III; Act III, Scene I; Act V, Scene I.

calls her "Shakespeare's first holy Christian woman," and Mrs. Jameson could not say enough in praise of "the strong undercurrent of passion and enthusiasm flowing beneath this calm and saintly self-possession . . . the capacity for high feeling and generous and strong indignation, veiled beneath the sweet austere composure of the religious recluse."

Here in a group of comedies where the disguises, the concealed identities, the intrigues, and especially the moral slackness of the later drama appear in force and seem for a time almost to corrupt the fine imagination of Shakespeare (*Measure for Measure, All's Well That Ends Well,* and *Pericles*), the atmosphere of sin and death is to a great degree balanced by the superb beauty of the heroine's character. In *Hamlet*, as all men know, there is a scant reference to a nunnery; in *A Midsummer Night's Dream* there is a passage which gives the lie to the anachronistic phrase of "love-lacking vestals and self-loving nuns"; in *Venus and Adonis*, a passage which, though delivered as a threat, is a strong and alluring tribute:

> You can endure the livery of a nun,
> For aye to be in shady cloister mew'd,
> To live a barren sister all your life,
> Chanting faint hymns to the cold, fruitless moon.
> Thrice blessed they that master so their blood,
> To undergo such maiden pilgrimages.[19]

Though the nun Francisca is allowed to speak but nine short lines in her Viennese convent and these to tell of the re-

[19] *A Midsummer Night's Dream,* Act I, Scene I.

strictions put upon the inhabitants, the novice compensates amply by the character Shakespeare has made her display, a character resulting from her pious training as well as from her own heart of gold. Professor J. S. P. Tatlock has been at some slight pains in a footnote to ridicule those critics who complain that the Duke decides on marriage for the novice without consulting the Mother Superior,[20] but the broad firmness of her character makes such answers, if not the complaints themselves, unnecessary. "Isabella has the innate dignity which renders her 'queen o'er herself,' but she has liv'd far from the world and its pomps and pleasures; she is one of a consecrated sisterhood—a novice of St. Clare. . . . Isabella is like a stately and graceful cedar, towering on some alpine cliff, unbowed and unscathed amid the storm. She gives us the impression of one who has passed under the ennobling discipline of suffering and self-denial; a melancholy charm tempers the natural vigor of her mind; her spirit seems to stand upon an eminence, and look down upon the world as if already enskied and sainted; and yet when brought in contact with that world which she inwardly despises, she shrinks back with all the timidity natural to her cloistral education. This union of natural grace and grandeur with the habits and sentiments of a recluse—of austerity of life with gentleness of manner—of inflexible moral principle with humility and even bashfulness of deportment—is delineated with the most beautiful and wonderful consistency. . . . There is a profound yet simple morality, a depth of religious feeling, a touch of melancholy, in Isabella's sentiments, and something earnest and authoritative in the manner and ex-

[20] *Sewanee Review*, April, 1916, p. 142 *n.*

pression, as though they had grown up in her mind from long and deep meditation in the silence and solitude of her convent cell."[21]

The last play of Shakespeare's which we shall consider is the most important in that it illustrates the poet's religious attitude toward the broad things of life. Yet it is so well known and has so often been recited, read, presented, that there is scant need for discussion. A few suggestions concerning it will indicate the trend of this paper and of the mind of Shakespeare as regards religion, for *Hamlet* is almost universally acknowledged as the ripe mature product and consummation of both the philosophic mind and the theatric art of the world's greatest dramatic writer. We have already made mention of a few minor points wherein this play of the royal Dane is in conformity with the doctrine and the ritual of Catholicism. And all the world knows the scene at the grave of Ophelia, poor, mad, drowned Ophelia, and the prominence given there to the matter of the "rites of the Church."

But it is in a larger sense that we shall look on the worried face of Hamlet. *Hamlet* is the end, both of this essay and of the mounting genius of Shakespeare. When we have said the last word about it, we have said the last word about Shakespeare. Schlegel has said of the Prince of Denmark that after he first follows the ghost of his murdered father and holds the hilt of his sword before him as protection against the mischance of a spirit damned, that after this preliminary interview, if you will, "from expressions of religious confidence he passes over to skeptical doubts." And some have been so mad as to call Prince Hamlet mad.

---

[21] Mrs. Jameson, *Characteristics of Women*.

## Clerical Characters in Shakespeare 135

As a matter of fact, the play is not like *Love's Labours Lost* to cure the world of pride, nor like *The Merchant of Venice* to cure it of religious vindictiveness, nor like *Lear* to show how sharper than a serpent's tooth it is to have an ungrateful child, nor like *Macbeth* to indicate the evil of insinuating ambition and superstition, nor like *Othello* to deplore unwarranted jealousy, nor like *Romeo and Juliet* to show the folly of senseless feuds. It is the plain picture of a Christian soul struggling with terrible temptation, the desire to avenge combating with an abhorrence of a deed of horror. Hamlet is tormented by his conscience. Courtier, scholar, soldier, his final victory is a real defeat, for he accomplishes the act of murder. Then and not earlier would it have been time for Ophelia to say

> Oh, what a noble mind is here o'erthrown!

This is the tragedy of Hamlet, the tragedy resulting from a broken law. Up to the end each character has sinned save only the Prince; Rosencranz and Guildenstern were treacherous toward their friend and retribution overthrew them; Polonius was an intriguing spy and died ingloriously like a rat; Ophelia did not understand and could not help, so guiltless she had to be set aside; Laertes stooped to villainy and died poisoned by his own sword; the Queen was unfaithful and fell by chance; the King bore the chief guilt and his overthrow was the most haunting and the most dramatic; he was "justly served." At the close, Hamlet runs his sword into the King and all the wicked plotting has combined to crush him just as his aim is accomplished. He was a Christian and did a deed of violence, so he died. His material triumph in ascending the throne is marred by his spiritual failure in dabbling in sin. The failure returns upon him, and his life as well as the play is a tragedy.

Opposed to Hamlet is his friend Horatio, "more an antique Roman than a Dane," a philosopher out of the university, a skeptic, a man of book learning with little passion and much knowledge. The strong spirit of the Danish Prince uses him as a foil where Horatio should have turned the thoughts of revenge aside, or at least tried to. But all the mind could not make up for the lack of heart. Rosencranz and Guildenstern could trifle with words, but, since philosophic explanations are tortuous as well as difficult, could never cope with the simplicity of a Christian soul under temptation. Horatio had not the wit to turn aside the rising emotions and straighten out the world that then was out of joint, as Father Brown or Friar Francis might have done. Here was something primitive and not primary, elemental and not elementary. He knew not how to interpose a helpful hand. Truly,

> There are more things in heaven and earth, Horatio,
> Than are dreamt of in your philosophy.

# 8

# Two Religious Poets

## *Southwell and Crashaw*

AT THE end of the period of isolations, small communities, and struggles which has been called the Middle Ages; after Constantinople fell and learned scholars scattered the learning of classical times across the face of Europe, travel became more general and the reading of books more widespread. This has been called the Renaissance. The vernacular languages began to have literatures. The introduction of the process of mechanical printing had much to do with this, even though prior to Caxton and for centuries after his time the circulation of works in manuscript copies, many times copied and recopied, was universal. Poems were composed for pleasure, the pleasure of the author and the pleasure of his friends. Reading increased, and as writing increased it bore ever-increasing signs of the reading which had preceded it. Bursting practically into its full flower with Tottel's *Miscellany* in 1557, the Renaissance was upon England. It brought the poesy and the narrative of France and Italy, and nurtured their imitators.

This Renaissance poetry of the Continent had two significant phases. There was in it a richness of allusion to literature and a striving for fantasy in language. Villon's recital of the names of the ladies of long ago illustrates the beginning of one phase:

> Tell me where in what land of shade
> Bides fair Flora of Rome, and where
> Are Thaïs and Archipiade,
> Cousins-german of beauty rare?

Marlowe's: "Thou art fairer than the evening air, clad in the beauty of a thousand stars," illustrates the other, even though it be richer in its simplicity and later in its date. This poetry of which we chiefly speak was written for a certain society convention, in praise of a lady, out of love and with an effort to create a perfection of compliment. One able scholar has even seen in it a "religion of beauty in woman"—and the beauty was supposed to be as much of the mind as of the flesh. To appeal to the high mind of a witty woman, poets attempted to outdo themselves. Compliments became more and more extravagant. It was so in Italy, where the "conceits" of Petrarch were succeeded by the distortions of Marino. It was so in England, too. In its finest examples the sonnets of Shakespeare typify its perfection of compliment. But the sonnets of Shakespeare are relatively restrained in their language, fanciful without being fantastic. Most of the poetry of this age seems strange and unnatural to us today. Its effort to utilize—if not to display—the wealth of words at its author's command divides the attention and impedes the action. The extravagance of Lyly's *Euphues* is to us distortion. We prefer the simpler speech of Shakespeare. And yet it is to be noted that the men who were nearest to us in temper and in direct simplicity of image, Shakespeare ("All the world's a stage"), Marlowe ("Stand still ye ever-moving spheres of heaven!"), and Ben Jonson ("Drink to me only with thine eyes!") were not purely courtly poets. Through the drama they touched the common folk and held closer to reality. Even the courtly verses of Ben Jonson, rich with the power of learning and with transformed epigrams of Vergil, Horace, and Martial, were not distorted reflections. The old ideas were made his own, human in their simple images. Thus they have lived.

In those days when life was becoming an extravagance alive, when show was piled on show, richness on richness, it was considered in high intellectual circles proper to multiply metaphor and belabor an idea with a succession of similes. We see this most familiarly perhaps in Portia's speech to Shylock on the quality of mercy. In other work it is strained and unfamiliar. As Dr. Samuel Johnson has pointed out, the poets sought for nicety of distinction, for combinations of images, for linguistic dissection of every idea until not a bit of it was alive. This was the main characteristic, and perhaps the historical origin, of those whom Dr. Johnson called "a race of writers that may be termed the metaphysical poets." Courthope has a wide definition for this "race" which would include the "easy natural Suckling" whose cynical mind could "hate a fool that starves her love only to feed her pride," and—far distant— the "holy ever-living lines" of George Herbert. It was conscious writing. Herrick said:

> Better 'twere my book were dead
> Than to live not perfected.

It was artificial writing, inventing words, creating extravagant hyperbole, and piling on successive paradoxes. Novelty of phrase appeared more desirable than bright truth. From the fantasy of costume where every poetic lover was a shepherd, English verse moved into the fantasy of phrase where every writer was an inventor of metaphor. At the same time prose was being whipped from the rambling antithetical extravagances of *Euphues* into the short, sculptured condensations of Francis Bacon: "Reading maketh a full man, conference a ready man, writing an exact man." Such work does not flow spontaneously with the lilt of song. It is consciously wrought into the shape the author intends. The product of this shaping was in those days considered "Wit." Although Alexander Pope was not of this school, his lines define it:

> True wit is Nature to advantage dressed,
> What oft was thought, but ne'er so well expressed.

Dr. Garnett called it: "the exaggerated art of men attempting to surpass the artistic perfection of their predecessors." This "Wit" is said by Courthope to be of three classes, "metaphysical" or "theological" or "court" wit. The latter is nearer our idea of wit than the others; to understand the others we must realize the classical, scholastic, and renaissance reading of these writers. We must take this background before we can understand the writings and appreciate the skill of those men whose writings are to us—so accustomed to the pictorial simplicity and the pure emotionalism of modern verse—so complicated and repetitious.

I

## Robert Southwell

Into such a literary world introduce a fine young man as fully versed in Latin authors, classical and more recent, as his years and his leisure would allow. Acquaint him with the best authors of his own language. Give him a consuming passion and devote his life to it alone. The result is an intensity of feeling in his chosen field which raises the wordiness of his letters to the exaltation of undying verse. The result is Robert Southwell, poet and martyr, who eschewed the practice of other poets who were "abusing their talents and making the follies and faynings of love the customarie subject of their base endeavours" and wrote poems of deep religious feeling which show "how well verse and virtue suit together." Here is no mere trickery of phrase. The passion of the man burns more brightly than the scintillations of his art. His repetitions have all the power of solemnly chanted litanies. His work is consequently read, as Thurston says, "not merely for the sake of his poetry, but for the spiritual food the poems contained." It conforms to the true nature of art, to capture and perpetuate an excellent and elemental mood. It is to secure such that men have ever, and ever will, turn their minds and eyes from the contemporary scene to the exaltations of high literature.

Born in 1561–62 at Horsham, St. Faith's near Norwich, Robert Southwell was son of a property holder, grandson of a Privy Councillor, great-grandson of an official of the

Exchequer under Henry VIII. His family was one of the "great army" of Catholics in England and sent him to the English College at Douay and then to Paris. In the latter city, he studied under the exiled Thomas Derbyshire, who joined the Society of Jesus, that remarkable organization which was so influential in the purging of abuses from Catholicism and in the world-wide propagation of the True Faith. The young Southwell also burned to become a Jesuit, and chafed that his extreme youth caused delay. Not content to remain in Paris, he went to Rome and there on October 17, 1578, entered the Jesuit Novitiate. It has been said that he desired the triple crown of "virginity, learning, and martyrdom," and Sister Rose Morton's appreciative thesis goes so far as to say that such was "his personal ambition." She adds: "How much the idea possessed his heart and mind may be gleaned from his letters to his friends as well as from his personal notes. It was almost the beginning and end of every sentence."

After two years as a novice at Tournay, he returned to Rome for his philosophy and theology and there secured a thorough classical training. We know from external evidence that his studies in Latin and Greek took him deeply into Cicero, Ovid, Vergil, Tibullus, Catullus, Homer, Plato, the Latin Fathers, St. Basil, St. Chrysostom, Gregory Nazianzus, and the Gospels. He was a brilliant student. Ordained at Rome in 1584, he was immediately made prefect of studies at the English College and, if we may judge from his appointment to this post and from the quality of his later writing, must have mastered his own language, studied the best English authors, and achieved thorough facility with his native tongue.

Two years later, upon his own application and "to his great joy" he was assigned to duty on the mission to England. Catholicism was being martyred by the red hand of Queen Elizabeth. Father Campion had been executed at Tyburn. Laymen were being coerced or frightened into conformity. Clerics were hounded. Mass was forbidden. Priests ordained since Elizabeth's first year were barred from remaining in England more than forty days on pain of a painful death. However, there were still English Catholics spiritually starving for the comforts of their religion and still priests like Southwell eager to risk torture and martyrdom to serve their people. Southwell's very father had weakened in his faith. The youth was burning "for the opportunity to lay down his life and was greedy for the rack and the gallows." He landed in disguise on July 7, 1586. For six years he traveled tirelessly, and always surreptitiously up and down the country "preparing an abundance of the Bread of Angels for the repast of persecuted Catholics."

Finally betrayed by the apostate and degenerate daughter of a staunch Catholic family, the Bellamy's of Uxenden Hall, Father Southwell in 1592 fell into the hands of the notorious Topcliffe, informer extraordinary and torturer most vicious, who told the Queen: "I never did take so weighty a man." In his own house, the villainous Topcliffe confined and tortured his prisoner in many ways, one of which consisted in hanging him up by the wrists in circles of iron, and leaving him there for hours at a time, but never getting him to whisper even a word which might reveal who were his friends and helpers. Sir Robert Cecil's descriptive words are immortal: "Let antiquity boast of its

Roman heroes, and the patience of captives in torments: our own age is not inferior to it, nor do the minds of the English cede to the Romans. There is at present confined one Southwell, a Jesuit, who, thirteen times, most cruelly tortured, cannot be induced to confess anything, not even the color of the horse whereon, on a certain day, he rode, lest from such indication his adversaries might conjecture in what house or in company of what Catholics, he that day was."

After four months, he was removed from Topcliffe's to Gatehouse and there neglected in filth for a month, until upon a visit and a petition by his father to the Queen, "as he was a gentleman," he was removed to the Tower and permitted to be supplied with clothing and books. It has generally been assumed that while thus in prison Father Southwell wrote his poetry. On this subject Pierre Janelle in his *Robert Southwell the Writer*[1] says: "Not a single one of his extant poems was composed after the date of his capture, May 26, 1592; not a single one of them was written in the Tower. Father Garnet's statement to the effect that he had neither ink nor paper during his imprisonment[2] settles the question finally."

[1] London (1935). Quotations by permission of Sheed and Ward, publishers.
[2] Southwell was kept in rigid isolation, but Father Garnet succeeded in having a breviary taken to him. When after Southwell's death this breviary was returned Garnet found that the only writing in it had been done with pin scratchings. The name of "Jesus" could thus faintly be read and the words, "My God, and my All." Many numbers were similarly scratched in, which probably pertained to his examination of conscience. But there was not one single sign made with ink, from which Garnet concludes he was never granted this commodity so that he might not write to his friends. Cf. *Robert Southwell the Writer*, p. 69.

Two poems only, Janelle believes, can be dated with certainty from contemporary events: one which must have been written soon after the death of Mary, Queen of Scots (February 8, 1587), *Decease, Release,* etc., and the other which must have been composed soon after Philip Howard was condemned to death (April 14, 1589), *I die without desert.* The *Triumphs over death* and the lives prefixed to it must have been written before September 30, 1591.[3]

Early in 1595 the trial of Southwell took place. He himself petitioned for a trial, and Cecil said "if he was in so much haste to be hanged, he should have his desire." He was forthwith removed to Newgate for three days and thence to Westminster "brought along with halbuts and bills and his arms tied with a cord" for a trial from which there could be but one outcome. Dragged to Tyburn on a hurdle, on a day when the hanging of a notorious highwayman was announced for another part of town to draw away the crowds, he was mounted on the gallows, allowed to say a few gracious and pious words, bunglingly hanged by a badly adjusted noose, cut down when dead, decapitated and quartered. "His head was set on one of the bridges and his quarters on the four gates of London."[4] Charles Blount, Eighth Baron Montjoy, who saw him die, said: "Pray God, whensoever I die, that my soul may be with this man's."

Robert Southwell at the age of thirty-three had achieved martyrdom, and his pen as well as his soul had attained the lofty level of immortality. His works were mostly published after his death, in 1595, in various little pamphlets, and have been repeatedly "collected" and reprinted ever

[3] *Ibid.,* pp. 160 and 161.   [4] Morton, *op. cit.,* p. 36.

since, right down to our own day. Since their publication some of them have been found in every major collection of the canon of English verse. One was Ben Jonson's favorite and learned by heart. Their popularity has been ascribed to the dual incidence of their purely religious motives and to the vast number of ardent Catholics still in England at that time. They may not be suited for "general" reading or for wide acceptance in later times, but their author's name is not "writ in water" for the simple reason that they are superlative art. They achieve eminence by the perfect manner in which they fulfilled the task to which the poet set himself when he wrote them, to capture a sentiment and shape it deathlessly, a sentiment "of higher things for higher ends." Others might write for pleasure of the populace or the pleasantry of the court, but, as Professor Schelling says of the Elizabethans, "Southwell alone devoted his muse *in toto* to the praise and glory of God." He avoided many of the current extravagances, Italianism, pastoralism, but not the "conceits," wrote in old-fashioned meters and was a true disciple of the lyrical Philip Sidney. Let us look for a moment at an inferior Catholic poet of his time, at Chidiock Tichborne, who writes:

> My prime of youth is but a frost of cares;
> My feast of joy is but a dish of pain;
> My crop of corn is but a field of tares;
> And all my good is but vain hope of gain;
> The day is fled, and yet I saw no sun;
> And now I live and now my life is done.

Tichborne was also a Catholic martyr. The lines quoted are obviously antithetical in the most extreme Euphuist convention. They illustrate the use of alliteration and assonance so common in the conscious writing of that age. They give, however, such an accumulation of metaphors in such a narrow compass and so unrelated, that no vivid image remains, not even the resignation of the author or his distaste for the vanities of the world. With them it is not unfair to compare somewhat similar lines from Southwell:

> For that I love I long, but that I lack;
>     That others love I loathe, and that I have;
> All worldly freights to me are deadly wrack;
>     Men present hap, I future hope do crave;
> They, loving when they live, long life require;
> To live where best I love, death I desire.

Read this slowly. Modernize it with a "what" instead of the first "that" in each of the first two lines. Slowly read, it is deep in its emotion, powerful in its saintly wish to be with God. It has the alliteration, the assonance, just as Tichborne's verse did, but it lacks the profusion of wasteful imagery, and is truer in its representation of feeling. A stanza like this makes one say that in Southwell passion transcends the mere artistry of his age. It is true that at times he lets his words run away with him, as when he makes Queen Mary say:

> From crown to cross, from throne to thrall I fell;
>     My right my ruth, my titles wrought my trap,
> My weal my woe, my worldly heaven my hell.

Yet there was fervid imagination and powerful exaltation

in the mind and soul of the man who could write *The Burning Babe:*

> As I on hoary winter's night stood shivering in the snow,
> Surprised I was with sudden heat, which made my
>     heart to glow;
> And lifting up a fearful eye, to view what fire was near,
> A pretty babe all burning bright did in the air appear,
> Who, scorched with excessive heat, such floods of tears
>     did shed,
> As though His floods should quench His flames which
>     with His tears were fed;
> "Alas!" quoth He, "but newly born in fiery heats I fry,
> Yet none aproach to warm their hearts, or feel My fire,
>     but I!
> My faultless breast the furnace is, the fuel wounding thorns;
> Love is the fire, and sighs the smoke, the ashes shame and
>     scorns;
> The fuel Justice layeth on, and Mercy blows the coals;
> The metals in this furnace wrought are men's defiléd souls,
> For while as now on fire I am, to work them to their good,
> So will I melt into a bath to wash them in My blood."
> With this He vanished out of sight, and softly shrunk away,
> And straight I called unto my mind that it was Christmas
>     day.

This poem leaves one with an indelible picture, and therein lies its greatness. It commences with a simple man and ends with a simple fact. Did you ever imagine the heat of a halo around the saint's head? The poet has visualized the warm glow of the bright light which surrounds a painted picture of the Immortal Child. Grant that he trips into the alliterations of his age. Grant that his figures of speech are crowded. Look at a similar painting some time and let your imagination run. . . . This is the work of a poet, and a poet of a particular age. It is also superior poetry because it has form in its broader sense, a symmetry of its rounded thought as well as of its verbal line. Francis Bacon once got from Topcliffe a writing by Southwell, his *Humble Supplication* of 1591, and told his brother it was "worth the writing out for the art." This poem is art in its larger aspects, just as a painting may be art not only by reason of its technique, but also by reason of its representation of worthy ideas and of its effect upon men within whose ken it comes, by reason of the thoughts it stirs. It has its complications to be sure; yet it also has its powerful, direct, and simple appeal. It leaves an imprint upon the memory as everlastingly as Rupert Brooke's "bit of soil that is forever England," as Alan Seegar's "rendezvous with death at some disputed barricade," as Tennyson's last desire to sail "beyond the sunset," as Wordsworth's "light that never was on sea or land," as even Whitman's lilacs last in the dooryard blooming or his thoughts and acts when he heard the learned astronomer tangle a universe with words and then went out and looked up at the stars.

In addition to several shorter lyrics, Robert Southwell wrote what may be called a "sequence" beginning with the Immaculate Conception and ending with incidents at the Crucifixion, and also a long piece of nearly eight hundred lines, *St. Peter's Complaint*, which approaches religion, Gethsemane, and the Crucifixion from every possible angle. This last has often been cited as a too-long-drawn-out extravaganza, as attempting to find literary similes and fanciful images for too many a minor incident, Peter's drawing of the sword, warming himself by the fire, enduring the gaze of Christ. Such may be just criticism, but this is the poem which should be read as a litany. Peter speaks to Christ, confessing his faults and asking for pity and love. Apostrophe it is indeed, as much of prayer is apostrophe. Its ramifications but illustrate the frantic gropings of a sorrowing soul, acknowledging sin and hardly daring to ask forgiveness. It is a succession of moods, and on that account criticized. It cannot of course be called great, but it should not of course be condemned. It was trying to be as tortuous as it is condemned for being, as frantic as it has been called fantastic. It reads faint and far away to the modernist schooled in the romantic simplicity of the last century. One should never couple it with the present age. The poem should be read slowly, with a contrite spirit recreating the anguish of a troubled heart:

> My eyes read mournful lessons to my heart,
>   My heart doth to my thought the grief expound;
> My thought the same doth to my tongue impart,
>   My tongue the message in the ears doth sound;
> My ears back to my heart their sorrows send;
> Thus circling griefs run round without an end.

It is penitential piety of an emotional sort. It was written by a man who looked forward to being slaughtered for his faith's sake. It has the frantic imagery of a mind without restraint, and utilizes to the full the license of the age for far-fetched imagery. Understood thus, even its much-abused succession of verses should be received with a new understanding.

# Robert Southwell

To his shorter poems, a commentary like this cannot do full justice. It is possible, however, to point out one fact. *Mary Magdalen's Complaint at Christ's Death* is one of the finest religious poems in English, rich in feeling and apt in phrase, poignant in its thought although it clings to complex metaphor:

> Silly stars must needs leave shining
>   When the sun is shadowed,
> Borrowéd streams refrain their running
>   When head springs are hindered.
> One that lives by other's breath
> Dieth also by his death.

Those who cannot raise their moods to meet the exalted strain of such verse as this, who desire something more modern and simple, may turn to the poem *New Prince, New Pomp* and read of a freezing winter night when a tender babe trembling lay in a homely manger:

> Weigh not his crib, his wooden dish,
>   Nor beasts that by him feed;
> Weigh not his mother's poor attire,
>   Nor Joseph's simple weed.
> This stable is a prince's court,
>   The crib his chair of state;
> The beasts are parcel of his pomp,
>   The wooden dish his plate.
> With joy approach, O Christian wight,
>   Do homage to thy King;
> And highly praise this humble pomp,
>   Which he from heaven doth bring!

It is so with the verse of Southwell. The wise men bearing gifts from the East were not deterred by externals. They sought the spirit and found it exalted and rare. So, in approaching the poems of Robert Southwell, we must make our allowances, allowances for the conventions of his age, for the tricks of literature in those days, for the utter fervency of his martyr soul. They are religious verses, not the love lyrics of a Shelley or the reasoned rhymes of an Alexander Pope. Read them for their religious mood, and their exaltation will stamp them fully into the aspirations of your soul. No man who reads *The Burning Babe* attentively even once, will ever forget it.

II

## *Richard Crashaw*

Our other great poet of this troubled century in England was born almost a full score of years after Southwell died. He wrote some half a century later. Britain's religion had been Anglicized and was in the process of being simplified and leveled into drab Puritanism. His own father was a Puritanical clergyman, given to anti-Catholic and anti-Jesuit writings. Richard Crashaw was born in London in 1612–13, lost his mother early, lost his stepmother in 1620, and his father in 1626. His education commenced at the Charterhouse and was continued at Cambridge in 1631. Here he wrote Latin epigrams, mastered many languages and—at Peterhouse and St. Mary's Church—lived in a quasi-monastic manner a life of intense religious thought, together with several other pious souls, where he "offered more prayers in the night than others usually offer in the day."

In 1643, Puritan reforming soldiers and Parliamentary commissioners visited Cambridge, destroyed statuary, broke up the community, and sent Crashaw out into the world when, as a fellow of the University, he refused to sign the Solemn League and Covenant. He went to Oxford for a time, to London where he published his *Steps to the Temple* in 1646, became a Catholic, and left England forever. The same year he was found by his friend Cowley, in Paris and poor. Queen Henrietta Maria graciously helped him while he wrote his *Carmen Deo Nostro* (pub. 1652), and gave him letters to Italy where he went in 1649 to become private secretary to Cardinal Palotto, Governor of Rome. In 1650 he started for Loretto, fell sick on the road and died a few weeks after arriving at his new church, where he still rests in eternal peace after a troubled life.

Such was the career of one of the truest lyrists in the English language. Although it has been customary to speak of his early, profane verse and to quote lines to his supposed mistress:

> That not impossible she,
> That shall command my heart and me.

the topic should be lightly passed over. Such verse from his pen was inconsequential, in amount and in quality. He could not write "on a less subject than Eternity," and when he wrote on that and upon its earthly manifestations, he wrote indeed. His emotional temperament resounded in sustained song which gives us many of the finest singing lines in literature. He was an imitator, perhaps, of George

Herbert, whose "Temple" Crashaw followed with "Steps to the Temple." The age was one of allegory. It is seen in *Pilgrim's Progress* and in *Paradise Lost*. It appears in most of the metaphysical poets. It was purely such in Francis Quarles' *Emblems*, each a fantasy on a single fact. We find its worst traits and its best together in George Herbert, his picture of "God with a glass of blessings standing by" and in his saying that "the dew shall weep the fall of day." Into some of such excesses Crashaw fell. Of his poem *The Weeper* it has been said: "No metrical composition in the English language of the same length contains so much imagery and so little thought."

Richard Crashaw had the fervor of Southwell. He had the imagery. He was emotional where Southwell was the more intellectual. But we have not dismissed Crashaw when we say such things as this. Verse of those dimensions does not place a man forever among the foremost English poets, a place where Crashaw is acknowledged to stand. As Edmund Gosse remarked: "The custom of his age permitted the use of images and phrases which we now justly condemn as incongruous and unseemly, and the fervent fancy of Crashaw carried this license to the most rococo excess. At the same time, his verse is studded with fiery beauties and sudden felicities of language. There is no religious poetry in England so full at once of gross and awkward images, and imaginative touches of the most ethereal beauty."

We have seen it held that Southwell was descended from the same Shelley family which two centuries later produced the great Shelley. With him, Southwell has nothing in common, although of distant kinship. With him, Crashaw is inevitably tied by the quality and touch of his genius, the "ease and music of his lines," and what Professor Schelling has called "the atmosphere of light and radiance that pervades the best of his poetry." The ecstasy is not merely of the mind and soul. It is of the heart. There is often a lift to his verse like that of Shelley's blithe skylark spirit. His verse is simpler than Southwell's, less heavy with ideas, more lilting in its movement. He can, at his best, produce a sustained lyric quality that is rare in any poetry. Robert Southwell was worried in his heart, aching for heaven. Crashaw is happy in his song, and the happiness is reflected in the swing of his words. He can versify:

>     Dear, heav'n-designéd soul!
>         Amongst the rest
>     Of suitors that besiege your maiden breast,
>         Why may not I
>         My fortune try
>     And venture to speak one good word
>     Not for myself, alas! but for my dearer Lord?

> \* \* \*

>     'Tis time you listen to a braver love,
>         Which from above,
>     Calls you up higher,
>         And bids you come
>         And choose your room
>     Among his own fair sons of fire,
>         Where you among
>         The golden throng,
>     That watches at his palace doors,
>         May pass along
>     And follow those fair stars of yours.

He can indulge in the elaborated figures of speech of the simile-seeking metaphysical school, as he does when he calls a prayer book, "in one choice handful, heaven," and then goes on to say:

> It is love's great artillery,
> Which here contracts itself, and comes to lie
> Close couched in their white bosom; and from thence
> As from a snowy fortress of defence,
> Against their ghostly foe to take their part,
> And fortify the hold of your chaste heart.
>
> It is an armoury of light;
> Let constant use but keep it bright,
>    You'll find it yields
> To holy hands and humble hearts,
>    More swords and shields
> Than sin hath snares, or hell hath darts.

He can do the successive figures and the litany, as in this oft-quoted passage from *The Flaming Heart*, inspired by the book and picture of "the seraphical Saint Teresa":

> O, sweet incendiary! Show here thy art
> Upon this carcass of a hard, cold heart;
> Let all thy scatter'd shafts of light, that play
> Among the leaves of thy large books of day,
> Combined against this breast, at once break in
> And take away from me myself and sin;
> This gracious robbery shall thy bounty be,
> And my best fortunes such fair spoils of me.
> O, thou undaunted daughter of desires!

> By all thy dower of lights and fires,
> By all the eagle in thee, all the dove,
> By all thy lives and deaths of love,
> By thy large draughts of intellectual day,
> And by thy thirsts of love more large than they;
> By all thy brim-fill'd bowls of fierce desire,
> By thy last morning's draught of liquid fire,
> By the full kingdom of that final kiss
> That seized thy parting soul, and seal'd thee his;
> By all the heavens thou hast in him,
> Fair sister of the seraphim!
> By all of him we have in thee,
> Leave nothing of myself in me:
> Let me so read thy life that I
> Unto all life of mine may die.

This we call true poetry, lyric of a superior level. Truly, "this to the ear speaks best." Real lyrics show the flow of easy words, the music of the sounds runs along so smoothly and so rapidly that we must pause a while here and there to let the sense sink in. The art of joining words here displayed is not the mere singing, jingling tintinnabulations of a Poe or the swinging alliterations of a Swinburne either. The lines of Crashaw have song, they have passion, in their very lift of phrase. They have imaginative metaphor as well. In the shaping of phrase, the incomparable Southwell is a mere logician by comparison, saved only by the emotion of his mind from the low level of prose. Here the sequences of syllables are lyric in themselves. As Edmund Gosse has said, such poetry England was not again to see until *Epipsychidion*. The singing trait would not reappear until it would be combined with the soft sentiments of Byron's best work, the mild melancholy of Tom Moore, and the passionate paganism of Shelley. After Crashaw, English verse turned to rolling numbers and merely splendid diction or into the sheer jog trot of Alexander Pope. For two hundred years, an England that repressed its emotions was not to hear lyrics like these.

# 9

# Three Seventeenth=Century Dramatists

## Shirley, Massinger, and D'Avenant

THE seventeenth century was a time almost unparalleled in the history of England and of its literature. During this period the Tudors departed and a Stuart was called down from subordinated Scotland to take the throne of Great Britain; the nation passed through trying civil dissension in the clash of arms and in parliamentary debate; one king was beheaded and another fled in terror of his life, later to see his crown declared vacant and a foreigner who spoke no English invited to wear its regal splendor. In the field of letters, the seventeenth century counts in the roll of its prized advocates the names of Shakespeare, Milton and Dryden—three of the greatest writers of all time. In 1600 the splendid flower of Elizabethan literature was but just breaking into bloom; at the end of a hundred years the scent was gone, the flower was remembered as a wild excrescence of nature, and conventionalized decoration had taken the place of spontaneous design, for whatever else it did, the Restoration did not restore an art that had died slowly and gradually.

In Massinger there are many remembrances of the fine old strength of "rare Ben Jonson"; in Shirley there was enough of the former fire left for a modern critic to remark with justice that "The Cardinal" was "the last great play produced by the giants of the Elizabethan age";[1] in D'Avenant the antique fashion is seen, but the new is making itself felt. "The old actors decay, the young sprout up."[2] But all was actually changing in the drama as well as in life.

> Marlowe is dead, and Greene is in his grave,
>   And sweet Will Shakespeare long ago is gone!
> Our Ocean-shepherd sleeps beneath the wave;
> Robin is dead, and Marlowe in his grave.
> Why should I stay to chant an idle stave,
> And in my Mermaid Tavern drink alone?
> For Kit is dead and Greene is in his grave,
>   And sweet Will Shakespeare long ago is gone.
>
> Where is the singer of the Faerie Queen?
>   Where are the lyric lips of Astrophel?
> Long, long ago their quiet graves were green;
> Ay, and the grave, too, of their Faerie Queen!
> And yet their faces, hovering here unseen,
>   Call me to taste their new-found oenomel;
> To sup with him who sang the Faerie Queen;
>   To drink with him whose name was Astrophel.[3]

This is a song which Massinger might well have sung. Shirley would have understood the sentiment, but would not have been so sorry. And D'Avenant would probably scarce-

---

[1] Edmund Gosse, in his preface to the "Mermaid" series.
[2] Massinger, "The Guardian" (1633).
[3] Alfred Noyes, *Tales of the Mermaid Tavern* (1913), p. 13. By permission of Frederick A. Stokes Co., publishers.

ly have understood. So it is that these three dramatists, taken in succession, well illustrate the trend of the English drama in these times.

I

## Shirley and Massinger

There is, however, one other thing which they had in common: they were all converts to the Catholic faith. And, since this essay is but one of a series on English Catholic men of letters, it shall not be inopportune to pause a while and comment on this strange coincidence. Philip Massinger[4] probably became converted to Catholicism while a student at Oxford. Whether or not this change in the opinions of this young man—who was possibly named for Sir Philip Sidney on account of his father's connection with the house of Pembroke—whether or not this change caused him to alter his ambitions and turn his pen from courtly success in distinguished circles to the art and business of playwriting we cannot say. The fact itself is obscure enough without inquiring into consequences. Indeed Professor Matthews has even gone so far as to call it a mere supposition based on passages in *The Renegade* and in *The Virgin Martyr*. The ground thus becomes more doubtful, for *The Virgin Martyr* (1620) was written in such close collaboration with Dekker that we cannot attribute passages save on supposition, and that play furthermore—though depicting the Roman persecutions of Christians in the matchless Dorothea's story—is really not characterized

[4] Born, 1584; died, 1640.

by any distinctly Catholic sentiments. Suffice it, then, merely to record the fact of his conversion, a fact to which almost all scholars have given ready and reasoned credence.

The conversion of Shirley[5] is less doubtful. Yet his recent scholarly biographer is not absolutely certain:

"Concerning his conversion to the Roman Church, we have only [the evidence] Dyce and other scholars [Gifford and Ward] have been pleased to discover in his dramatic works."[6]

Most students have been quite willing to admit validity to the tradition that, after stopping at Oxford and at Cambridge, he resigned (1624) a position as head master at St. Albans Grammar School on his conversion to Catholicism. A careful and thorough scholar has remarked:

"It may be said that a man who, in spite of attempts at dissuasion, enters the Church of England, and shortly after quits his profession and enters the Church of Rome, at a time when no possible advantage could accrue from his conversion, but, on the other hand, many inconveniences, shows a degree of thoughtfulness and conscientiousness which cannot help manifesting itself in his writings."[7]

And this same scholar has been at some pains to answer[8]

---

[5] Born, 1596; died, 1666, of terror and exposure resulting from the great fire of that year. He followed the Duke of Newcastle in the civil war, and then, after 1660, became a schoolmaster again.

[6] Arthur H. Nason, *James Shirley*, p. 32. This scholar, though, shows himself throughout his monograph a little meticulous in rendering judgments. Quotation by permission of the author.

[7] Quoted from Forsythe: *The Relation of Shirley's Plays to the Elizabethan Drama*, by permission of Columbia University Press. He also says: "Shirley seems to have been a favorite of Queen Henrietta Maria, perhaps, like Massinger, on account of his religion."

[8] *Ibid.*, pp. 57-59.

Charles Kingsley, who in *Plays and Puritans* attacks Shirley from "an evident desire to make out a strong case against the Anglican priest turned Papist and dramatist." Also it is entirely fruitless to remark that Edmund Gosse says, "It would seem, from a passage in 'The Grateful Servant,' that he was connected, as a Catholic, with the Order of Benedictines," and that others have been ready to accept this connection as at least that between a Catholic and his confessors. In addition we must take into consideration the "rumors that 'The Traitor' (his next best play to 'The Cardinal') was not the work of Shirley, but of a certain Mr. Rivers, a Jesuit."

The judgment of the best scholar in the Elizabethan field must not be forgotten nor disregarded, that of A. W. Ward:

"He nowhere puts himself forward as a combative Papist; but he loses no opportunity of exhibiting his attachment to the doctrines and practices of the creed professed by him (see 'The Wedding,' 'The Grateful Servant,' 'Love in a Maze'; with perhaps 'The Sisters'), and ridicules the popular prejudice against Rome alongside of that against Spain.[9] (See 'The Bird in a Cage.')"

And yet *The Cardinal* (1641) was scarcely the picture of a devout churchman by a loyal worshiper; it was in fact such a play of horror and violence as Beaumont and Fletcher themselves delighted to write. But even in this Shirley,

---

[9] Thomas Heywood's *Game of Chess*, for instance, catered to anti-Spanish sentiment so well that it elicited a formal protest from the Spanish Ambassador. The quotation is from Ward's "Critical Essay" in Gayly, C. M., *Representative English Comedies* (New York: 1913), Vol. III, p. 550. By permission of the Macmillan Co., publishers. The Gosse passage quoted above is from the introduction to the "Mermaid," Shirley, p. xi.

according to his usual practice, wars against "unjust acts" and "usurpation," and declares that in the Church can "only timely cure prevent a shame. Look on the Church's wounds!" These are not the words of an assailant, but the words of a reformer working from within. The situation is almost comparable to that in which William Langland issued his warning, to that in which a pope had to advise restraint to an over-ardent Philip of Spain, to that in which another pope later found need to warn James II of England against a too great zeal. For, in my own mind, there is no more doubt about the Catholicism of Shirley than there is about his acknowledged catholicity. He was in Ireland, probably from 1636 to 1640, under the patronage of George, Earl of Kildare, and though he wrote there for the same type of Protestant as at home, for an audience that, though it possibly contained "the matchless Orinda," was if anything more anti-Catholic than that in London, his chief work written for that Dublin stage was *St. Patrick for Ireland*.[10] And this was no British garrison drama! It is replete with miracles and conversions and the magic of Archimagus and the pagan priests and attempts to force St. Patrick from his missionary journey by means of poison and enraged snakes—all described with neat propriety. It is the tale of the coming of Christianity to Ireland:

> A man shall come into this land
> With a shaven crown, and in his hand
> A crooked staff; he shall command
> And in the east his table stand.
> From his warm lips a stream shall flow,

[10] Cf. Nason, p. 104.

## Shirley and Massinger

> To make rocks melt and churches grow,
> Where, while he sings, our gods shall bow,
> And all our kings his law allow.[11]

In our opinion, it was not by chance that this play contains some of the bravest poetry and the finest songs that Shirley has written, or that St. Patrick's final words are set in phrases of lasting worth. These two extracts may stand as fair examples. Thus he arrives:

> I came not hither
> Without command, legate from Him before
> Whose angry breath the rocks do break and thaw,
> To whose nod the mountains humble their proud heads.
> The earth, the water, air and heaven is His,
> And all the stars that shine with evening flames
> Show but their trembling when they wait on Him;
> This supreme King's command I have obey'd,
> Who sent me hither to bring you to Him,
> And this still wand'ring nation, to those springs
> Where souls are everlastingly refresh'd;
> Unto whose gardens whose immortal flowers
> Stain your imagin'd shades, and blest abodes.[12]

Thus he banishes the snakes and berates those who turned them against him by their magic art:

> In vain is all your malice, art, and power
> Against their lives, whom the great hand of heaven
> Deigns to protect. Like wolves, you undertake

[11] Act I, Scene 1.
[12] Act I, Scene 1.

A quarrel with the moon, and waste your anger;
Nay, all the shafts your wrath directed hither
Are shot against a brazen arch, whose vault
Impenetrable sends the arrows back
To print just wounds on your own guilty heads.[13]

The third of our dramatists, Sir William D'Avenant,[14] is said to have joined the Church of Rome when in exile in France, in 1645. He was across the channel with the royal refugees, and it is not without interest to discover that, after the great rebellion drove out him and other loyalists who fought for the King, he was appointed to succeed Lord Baltimore as Governor General of Maryland, presumably to strengthen the royalist cause in America. He sailed in 1650, but was captured by the soldiers of Cromwell and imprisoned successively in Cowes Castle and in the Tower, whence he was liberated in 1652. The facts here have seemed so clear that no one has searched for corroboration within his plays, among the uncertain fields of internal criticism.

His latest scholar-biographer, Professor Alfred Harbage of the University of Pennsylvania, whose *Sir William Davenant* has just appeared (1935), seriously questions the long accepted view of D'Avenant's conversion to the Catholic Faith, on the grounds that the contemporary biographer Aubrey made no mention of the conversion, that Anthony à Wood "may have been misled" by the French nationality and therefore apparently Catholic faith of D'Avenant's third wife, and that D'Avenant "was given

[13] Act V, Scene 3.
[14] Born, 1606; died, 1668.

# William D'Avenant

a Church of England burial" in Westminster Abbey. Beyond this Professor Harbage refuses to indulge in "debating the question" but does claim for D'Avenant "a kind of regretful agnosticism."

We find the Harbage argument not quite conclusive either and, for the time at least, prefer to follow the accepted view. If D'Avenant's conversion is perhaps more probable than that of Massinger, and less certain than that of Shirley, if his writing is less Catholic than that of Shirley, it is certainly less anti-Catholic than the *Assignation* and the *Spanish Friar* of Dryden—of the fact of whose conversion there is no question. D'Avenant was an important figure in the history of the English stage. He rounds out this chapter. We make no claim that his writing is typically Catholic as was Shirley's or Dryden's latest work. It is our desire merely to continue to follow the older opinion until further and more convincing facts are adduced than Professor Harbage presents.

So we shall conclude that our three dramatists were all Catholic, and converts.

II

## William D'Avenant

But far more important than their Catholicism was their undoubted achievement in the drama.

All three of these men were already successful writers of plays when Ben Jonson died, and all three show the influence of his great thesis. In the age of the Fletcherian comedy of vile emotions and unexampled falsehood in morals, characters, and action, they have learned some of the lessons that he taught. Although many of D'Avenant's early works are like those of Beaumont and Fletcher, there are at least three typically Jonsonian—*The Wits* (1634), *News From Plymouth* (1635), and *The Platonic Lovers* (1635), abounding in local character study almost verging on caricature and displaying the follies of his own age and country rather than the crimes of other lands and times. Shirley also reveals something of this vein in *A Witty Fair One* (1628), in *Hyde Park* (1632) and in *The Gamester* (1633). Massinger, however, is perhaps the nearest in thesis and in manner, as well as in point of time, to the great assailant of outrageous "humours." *A New Way to Pay Old Debts* (1633) is not merely like *The Silent Woman* (1612) by Jonson, and *A Trick to Catch the Old One* (1607), by Middleton—from both of which it was separated by a long space of years—a comedy of London middle-class intrigue; it is not merely an attack against the commercially minded *bourgeoisie* as represented in Sir Giles Overreach, "that's both a lion and a fox in his proceedings" and who held an unjust monopoly in the manufacture of gold and silver lace; it is in very intent a true Jonsonian comedy. And even though his play, *Believe As You List* (1631), had its scene in ancient Roman and Carthaginian times, it shows forth the struggle between the merchant and the prince, the middle class and the aristocrat, in such a manner that his audience could scarcely refrain from applying its situations to contemporary circumstances. But here he does not so much ridicule the commercial agents who were expanding the trade of the empire as he teaches potentates humility. His words concerning the ancients might well have been meant for an appreciation of the Merchant Adventurers themselves:

> These poor men,
> These Asiatic merchants whom you look on
> With such contempt and scorn, are they to whom
> Rome owes her bravery [outward splendor]; their industrious search
> To the farthest Ind, with danger to themselves,
> Brings home security to you unthankful ...
> ... These are indeed the nerves
> And sinews of your war, and without them
> What could you do?

However, more significant than this mere recognition of economic and social surroundings was the very manner in which these matters and manners were depicted. It was not for nothing that Massinger and Shirley were the friends of Jonson, though we are not sure how closely they were "sealed of the tribe of Ben." From him they caught something of the dignity and purpose of their art. In Massinger's play, *The Roman Actor* (1626), the author makes Paris defend on moral grounds both dramatic poetry and them "that search into the secrets of the time,"[15] and assail with fervent vigor those men who

> yet grudge us
> That with delight join profit, and endeavour
> To build their minds up fair, and on the stage
> Decipher to the life what honours wait
> On good and glorious actions, and the shame
> That treads upon the heels of vice.[16]

[15] Act I, Scene 3.   [16] Act I, Scene 1.

Massinger, like Jonson, was a conscious craftsman with a serious as well as a sober intent. When Fletcher and Middleton and Thomas Heywood were making virtue a flimsy declamation and cared little for real moral distinctions, Massinger and Shirley bore plainly in mind the great gap between right and wrong, as between light and darkness, and continually recalled it to the public by frequent attempts to differentiate upright, and shall we say downright, principles. Wickedness either dies absolutely or the wicked character dies. "In no play does wickedness go unpunished, if persisted in." Speaking of Shirley, Anthony à Wood wrote him down only a few decades after "the most noted dramatic poet of his time," and Forsythe more recently called this man "a writer who preferred morality (in the Caroline sense) and some degree of probability to originality and novelty." For, even though Shirley drew from literary convention rather than from life and ever found his source not in a single play, but in all the extravagant—and immoral—literature of his period, he never stooped to the worst excesses of that decadent and vulgar age. He was too much of an artist, and also too much of a moralist. And if he maintained a consistent level, perhaps —to borrow a phrase from Mr. Chesterton—we should not inquire too closely if the great plain was due to the absence of valleys or to the absence of mountains.

At any rate, we know that attempts at seduction were indignantly resisted *usque ad aras*, and that Shirley's more or less set speeches in praise of chastity ring more true than the shallower ones of his other contemporaries. In Massinger, too, there is little ribald morality or unreal virtuosity. The vicious die or reform and become virtuous. In

*The Guardian* (1633) even the bandits are good; in *The Fatal Dowry* (1632) a son goes himself to the debtor's prison to free his dead father's body for decent burial; and in *Believe As You List* (1631) Antiochus repels a courtesan even in prison. And when we consider the dates of these plays as well as the clear sincerity of the sentiments therein expressed, the attitude of the writers becomes more praiseworthy. It is the strength of a great mind. When Arthur Symons said that "Massinger is the late twilight of the long and splendid day of which Marlowe was the dawn," he was paying a deserved compliment to the author of *A New Way to Pay Old Debts*. Though the colors of sunset may make the world appear unreal, and though the strong light may be divided into the diverse rays of the spectrum, a great day usually ends gloriously, if not perfectly. And Shirley himself, the superb artist, whose tragedy, *The Cardinal*, shall ever stand among the first of English dramas, has long since outlived what Mr. Gosse calls "the unjust sneers of Dryden." Shirley and Massinger were great tragedians—unquestionably!—and in the field of comedy they toned down the Jonsonian product to such sensible limits that it was able to delight the British public for almost two centuries in a succession of plays which culminated in the power of Wycherley and the sparkling wit of Congreve and in the broader humor of Colman, Macklin, Cumberland, Dibdin, and Foster. Two centuries is not a short time!

D'Avenant, who catered to the public taste and so represents the changing fashions, has a literary history which extends in the annals of criticism all the way from the comedies of "humours" (which we have already mentioned),[17]

---

[17] *The Wits* (1634), *News from Plymouth* (1635) and *The Platonic Lovers* (1635).

through the flamboyant mode of Fletcher to the heroic play of the Restoration and Dryden, who collaborated with him and acknowledged him as a pioneer and master, and to the artificial and epigrammatical speech of Congreve. But the most noteworthy thing about D'Avenant is that he bridged the gap from the closing of the theaters in 1642 to their opening in 1660, in facts and in thought. His *Love and Honour* (1634) was a pseudo-heroic play concerning exactly what its title says, love and honor: it is close to the Fletcherian type, but geographically located in the direction of the heroic play. When the actors were again allowed to perform in London, D'Avenant received one of the two patents that were issued and opened his new house in Lincoln's Inn Fields with both parts of *The Siege of Rhodes* (1661),[18] true type of the heroic play in which the emphasis is changed:

For honor shall no leader have but love!

In his introductory epistle "To the Reader" D'Avenant indicates how the growing restrictions of the stage and the rules of the drama have caused a change from its antecedent —the early chronicle history play—to this type. He says: "The story represented is heroical, and notwithstanding the continual hurry and busy agitations of a hot siege, is (I hope) intelligibly convey'd to advance the characters of vertue in the shapes of valour and conjugal love. . . . The main argument hath but a single walk." Thus, in one of the first plays to use scenery extensively and the first to

[18] This had been acted in private in 1656.

have an Englishwoman act in an English play, we get very nearly the true characteristics of the heroic comedy: the elevated tone,[19] the superior maiden, the valiant hero who is yet jealous ("weakness, sprung from mightiness of love"), the battle on the stage (which had been omitted during the Fletcherian period), and the fall of kingdoms as a result of combat, not (as in Fletcher) as a result of courtly intrigue. For these reasons the method is called heroic. It deals with large international problems, not with petty political ones:

Villerius—
   "By armies, stor'd in fleets, exhausted Spain
   Leaves half her land unplough'd, to plough the main.
   And still would more of the old world subdue,
   As if unsatisfied with all the new."
Admiral—
    "France strives to have her lilies grow as fair
    In other realms as where they native are."
Villerius—
    "The English lyon ever loves to change
    His walks, and in remoter forrests range."
Chorus—
   "All gaining vainly from each other's loss;
   Whilst still the Crescent drives away the Cross."[20]

Villerius—
   "Let us no more by honor be beguil'd;
   This town can never be reliev'd;
   Alphonso and Ianthe being lost,
   Rhodes, thou dost cherish life with too much cost."

[19] "We'l for our crimes, not for our losses mourn."
[20] Part I, Act 2. Notice that the couplet is used.

Chorus—
> "Away, unchain the streets, unearth the ports,
>   Pull down each barricade
>   Which women's fears have made,
> And bravely sally out from all the forts!
> Drive back the Crescents, and advance the Cross,
> Or sink all human empires in our loss!"[21]

The chief characteristic of this play, as contrasted with *Love and Honour*, is typical of the changing taste. Now love is triumphant over honor, and honor is not so much a personal as a patriotic thing. It necessarily follows, then, that there should be some sort of a return to the genuine enthusiasm of former times.

In closing, therefore, we shall quote some vibrant lyric passages:

> Faire Evandra, the pride of Italy,
> In whom the graces met to rectifie
> Themselves that had not cause enough to blush
> Unlesse for pitty they were not so good
> As she; think now the easterne spices sweet,
> And that the blossoms of the spring perfume
> The morning ayre; necessity must rule
> Beliefe; let's strew our altars with them now,
> Since she's imprison'd, stifled, and chok'd up
> Like weeping roses in a still, whose inarticulate breath
> Heaven [thought] a purer sacrifice than all our orizons.[22]

---

[21] Part I, Act 4.
[22] *Love and Honour*, Act I, Scene 1.

Again:

>Give order that our troops march, march slowly on;
>Our drums should now in sable cases beate,
>Our collours foulded, and our muskets be
>Reverst, whilst our dejected pikes we traile. . . .
>O, Callandine! Evandra is in bonds![23]

And finally, some words out of the mouth of the Moslem monarch, Solyman the Magnificent:

>Our crescents shine not in the shade of night.
>But now the crescent of the sky appears.
>Our valour rises with her lucky light,
>And all our fighters blush away their fears.[24]

[23] *Love and Honour*, Act I, Scene 1.
[24] *The Siege of Rhodes*, Part II, Act 5, Scene 4.

# 10

## John Dryden

WE SCRUTINIZE a poet whose name is generally taken to designate his age. John Dryden, born in 1631, began serious composition almost at the exact date of the Restoration and died at the close of the century. Almost coincident with his death was the appearance of Congreve's *Way of the World*, which set a new dramatic fashion. Because of these accidental correspondences between his literary period and the space of years from the return of Charles II to the beginning of the new hundred years, it has been found convenient to speak of this time as "the age of Dryden." Yet the appellation must be granted much more of justice than the mere foundation of chance, for it can scarcely be questioned that Dryden absolutely dominated literary production during most of those forty years.

We are discussing, then, a man whose name will perhaps never die. Nevertheless, Dryden had a host of enemies and was as often blamed as praised. After graduating from Trinity College, Cambridge, and receiving the usual thorough classical education, we find him writing a poem to Cromwell in 1659, hailing the Lord Protector as a preserver of peace, as a creator of order out of chaos, and then, in 1660 (*Astræa Redux*), praising the return of the Stuarts and the royal establishment. These things were seized upon by later assailants as early instances of time-serving. But

Dr. Johnson replied to them: "The reproach of inconstancy was, on this occasion, shared with such numbers that it produced neither hatred nor disgrace; if he changed, he changed with the nation. It was, however, not totally forgotten when his reputation raised him enemies." And a more recent critic has pointed out that the "Lord Protector" poem merely praised the security made certain by Cromwell, not Cromwell himself, and that the praise of Charles II was therefore naturally due to a monarch who promised a further increase in governmental stability.[1]

Then when James II came to the throne Dryden became a Catholic, an action which drew on him more condemnations from his contemporaries,[2] but which was defended even by Dr. Johnson. Many other people have assailed Dryden on this score. They have pointed out that *Absalom and Achitophel* (1681), in spite of its famous line,

> Such an omniscient Church we wish indeed,

had compared the two religions to the advantage of the Anglican and the disadvantage of the Catholic. And they have pointed out also that *Religio Laici* (1682) and his stated change in religious belief concur very closely with what must at that time have been Dryden's material interest. On the death of D'Avenant he had succeeded to

---

[1] R. K. Root, "Dryden's Conversion to the Roman Catholic Faith," *Publications of the Modern Language Association*, 1907. Vol. XXII, pp. 298 ff.

[2] *The Reasons of Mr. Bays [Dryden] changing his Religion. Considered in a Dialogue between Crites, Eugenius and Mr. Bays.* By Thomas Brown, London, 1688.

the laureateship,³ and his interests and those of the court were very nearly identical.

Macaulay accused Dryden of changing his religion thus for material motives. Dr. Johnson and Scott considered the change due to fervent faith. George Saintsbury points out that Dryden "gained not one penny by his conversion," and says one should no more demand absolute consistency between his early and his late writings, as Macaulay does, than one should between the early and late opinions of Cardinal Newman. Mr. Root's judgment is that Dryden's real desire was political, for peace and order, which Cromwell brought to England, which the Anglican Church promised under Charles II, and which Dryden later came to believe might best be found where "only an infallible church can logically demand and enforce obedience."⁴

After his final conversion, Dryden continued, and died, a Catholic. Yet we cannot of course declare that all of his writing was Catholic.

We find several more incongruities in this matter. The first of these contradictory facts is the play *The Spanish Friar* (1681), an unchaste thing where religion and rogues go together and a huge, fat religious gentleman does things no Catholic sympathizer would make him do, a play which for its lewdness justly deserved the condemnation of Jeremy Collier, and lastly a play dedicated as "a Protestant play to a Protestant patron." In the same vein was *The Assignation; or, Love in a Nunnery* (1673), equally bad, of which, as Mr. Saintsbury has remarked, "nobody has

³ See "Dryden: Poet Laureate," *The Nation*, Vol. 98, p. 751.
⁴ Saintsbury, *Dryden*, pp. 102, 104; Root, *op. cit.*, p. 308.

ever been able to say much good."⁵ On the other hand is the obvious sincerity of a man who brought up three sons in the religion which he himself had embraced in middle age, and there is the fact that, when he professed Catholicism, he did not pretend to have changed in his conceptions of the fundamental doctrines of the Christian Church. Again, "we know that Dryden's several productions were so many successive expedients for his own support," and that *Religio Laici* was his only work which seems to have come from his heart and not from a calculating mind seeking for remuneration. There is no possibility of proving that Dryden would have lost by remaining an Anglican, nor that he actually gained by changing. He took a risk of losing by some new sudden change of royalties—as in fact he did lose his laureateship in 1689.⁶

I

Dryden's life was, in effect, rather a sad one. If in religious matters he kept his own counsel, in literary affairs he showed an almost malignant impatience. He assailed his assailants unremittingly, hesitating not to attack such, even of the nobility, as dared to attack him. Yet he was slowly supplanted on the dramatic stage by persons far inferior in ability and forced to devote much of his time to political satire. Nowadays a man asks: "Who was that man who

⁵ We may likewise cite Lyndaraxa's lines from *The Conquest of Granada* (1672), Part II, Act II, Scene 2, beginning "O Lottery of Fate," and a slighting reference to "ostentatious priests" in *Marriage à la Mode* (1673), Act IV, Scene 5.

⁶ I should go more deeply into the matter had not Mr. Root already done it before me.

quarreled with Dryden?" and when the answer comes, "Elkanah Settle!" inevitably all but professional literary historians have to query, "Who was he?" These were days of bitter literary feuds, in which personal attacks supplemented poetical asperities. For instance, Sir William D'Avenant had the ill luck to lose his nose, and was satirized on that account even by his friends. So one night as Dryden was returning from Will's Coffee House he was set upon and beaten by hired ruffians.

Thus, with the pen, Dryden gave blow for blow, buffet for buffet. *The Hind and the Panther* (1687) was as vigorous an attack as any man could want, and *The Medal* (1682) spared no feelings. In *MacFlecknoe* (1682), however, he passed to the extreme of abusiveness, for that poem was not merely an answer to Shadwell's repeated attacks upon his literary reputation, his political principles and his moral character, but stands as the acme of vindictiveness, after which the even more vindictive Alexander Pope was content to pattern his more famous, but more diffuse *Dunciad*.[7]

Times change and favor departs: the favor of courts and the constancy of public applause. As Sir Walter Scott has enumerated them, Dryden had to write and find commendation under three diverse British kings, "the needy Charles, who loved literary merit without rewarding it; the saturnine James, who rewarded it without loving it; and the phlegmatic William, who did neither the one nor the other." In years which stretched from the days of the Protectorate, through the reign of "the Merry Monarch" and that of the overzealous James, over "the glorious Revolu-

---

[7] See "Dryden in the Dunciad," *The Nation*, Vol. 98, p. 568.

tion" and into the establishment of the Hanoverian kings, Dryden lived and worked.[8] And finally when change of fortune drove him in turn even from the arena of poetical satire he turned to the art and business of translation. To him it was the art of translation, for in his many long prefaces, in the length of which he has scarcely been excelled except by Mr. Shaw, Dryden shows a clear consciousness of the difficulties and the dignities of his task. He establishes certain principles to which he tried to conform; no man was more exacting in his theories, which are still quoted with approval. To him it was the business of translation, for by it he had to earn the wherewithal to pay the butcher, the baker and the candlestick-maker. Scarcely has Charles Lamb's statement been better vindicated than by this gigantic example—that though literature may serve very well for a staff, it will hardly serve as a crutch. Many men in many ages have tried to live exclusively by what profit their pens might earn, and in most cases the declining years were tinged by the sadness of unproductive and exhausted genius which is harmed and harried by being continually urged on and on for mere pecuniary remuneration. Sheridan is a great example. In Dryden's own age, or to use a professorial phrase, in the Age of Dryden, Shirley spent his later years doing mere drudgework in translation for the bookseller Ogilby, and Elkanah Settle—who had an-

[8] Mr. Saintsbury's biography in the "English Men of Letters" Series, the articles in the *Dictionary of National Biography* and *The Cambridge History of English Literature* are replete in details. There is a more popular survey in a more recent book, *The Poets Laureate of England*, by W. Forbes Gray. Bibliographical data are to be found in the above, in *Catalogue of Dryden Exhibition* (1900), by the Grolier Club, in the introduction to the Everyman *Dramatic Essays*, and in "A Check List of Dryden's Plays" in *The Bibliographer*, November, 1902 (Vol. I, p. 374).

swered *Absalom and Achitophel* (1681) and *The Medal* (1682) with no mean success—died forgotten in a hospital after spending his declining years contriving shows for fairs and peddling occasional verses to families who could pay for commemorative poems on weddings or funerals. So with Dryden. Sick, discouraged, half-despised and half-forgotten, he died—by a strange irony for a pathetic scene—on May Day, 1701. No man may say exactly how much truth there is in the wild tale repeated by Congreve[9] concerning disputes and disagreements as to the manner and the circumstances of his burial. It may be true that these things happened as Congreve related them. It is at least true that he lay for a long time in an unmarked grave in Westminster Abbey until the Duke of Buckinghamshire gave him a tablet inscribed only with the name of DRYDEN.

II

The reputation which is attached to that name rests chiefly upon a few plays and upon a great many of which these few are the type. The "Restoration Drama" is characterized and dominated by Dryden. To appreciate him you must know the temper of the whole time, and in this century we are too forgetful of the days of the second Charles and the second James. It is, as Mr. P. P. Howe has said, a minor irony of our English-speaking theater that the drama called "Restoration" should be itself in need of restoration to favor. "It is more than a little ironic that the very plays with which the English theater broke its Puritan-imposed silence should be now the plays on which a silence is imposed."

[9] In his biography of Dryden.

## John Dryden

When the words of D'Avenant were being neglected, Dryden—who knew him as a collaborator[10] and revered him as a humble disciple should revere a master—continued the things which Sir William had revived, and established the type of the heroic play. In the preface to *The Conquest of Granada* (1672) he said: "Love and valor ought to be the subject," and then pointed out that the play that was heroic was but a stage representation of the already existing heroic poem. In the preface to *Aurengzebe* (1676) he even boasts that he has created the characters in that drama the nearest they could possibly be made to those of the heroic poem. D'Avenant used verse, but it was Dryden who boldly claimed, "Serious plays ought to be raised above the level of prose. . . . Heroic verse is already in possession of the stage."[11]

The main characteristics of these plays have already been seen in D'Avenant—to some degree at least—but they may be applied particularly to those which are most frequently cited as examples. There had been in the plays of Beaumont and Fletcher and in those of Shirley intrigues in high places, but it is not until we get to D'Avenant's *Siege of Rhodes* (1656), Dryden's *Conquest of Granada* (1672) and his *Aurengzebe* (1676) and to Otway's *Venice Preserved* (1682) that we see again the representation of battles and the frequent use of drums and trumpets which had existed in the early chronicle-history plays and in Shakespeare. Personal affairs are made to complicate international affairs, and ordinary amorous emotions to determine the

---

[10] See the adaptation of *The Tempest*, played November, 1667. The excellent phrasing of Mr. Howe is quoted from the New York *Times*, Dec. 15, 1912, p. 772.

[11] Preface to *The Conquest of Granada* (1672).

making and breaking of national allegiances as much in Dryden's *Conquest of Granada* (1672) as in D'Avenant's *Love and Honour* (1661). These, though, are not the mere allegories of the fall of princes or tragedies of the unfortunate great. The heroes are heroic, each is the soul of honor. Gone is the lascivious love of the early Jacobeans:

> Honor's the only idol of his eyes;
> The claims of beauty like a pest he flies.

The brotherly self-sacrifice in Otway's play, *The Orphan* (1680) is equaled if not outdone in *The Conquest of Granada* (1672), when Almanzor frees his captive Almahide, although he loves her, and when Boabdelin later frees his rival Almanzor, and gives him to the loving, but repining Almahide. That the notorious Nell Gwyn appeared in this play in a broad-brimmed hat and a waist-belt: not even this can detract from the heroic effectiveness of the ideal. The hero is superb, "the soul of honor," as I have said, and his conquering individuality stands forth like a bright comet against a midnight sky. He joins himself to the weaker side in combat, and the weaker side forthwith becomes the stronger. He is the subject for Henley's lines, he is the master of his fate:

> ... one great soul
> Whose single force can multitudes control.

And if he seems to boast too loudly at times of his own ability,

> The Moors have heaven, and me, to assist their cause,

he yet declares:

> If I am proud, 'tis only to my foes.

It is not ambition which drives him on; it is merely his unconquerable soul which bows to none and always upholds the right.

When finally this superhuman creature betrays one moral weakness, saying:

> Love has undone me,

he has revealed another characteristic of these plays. In them love is not a mere passion; it is a noble emotion, almost conforming to the definition of Ben Jonson, "the right affection of the mind, the noble appetite of what is best." Before the haughty heroine alone will he bow, the haughty heroine with alabaster brow and breast of stone. This lover's passion is a high and mighty sort of thing which interferes with the cause of nations, which coincides with the quest of honor at war without selfish ambition:

> Your beauty, as it moves no common fire,
> So it no common courage can inspire.
> As he fought well, so had he prospered, too,
> If, madam, he, like me, had fought for you.

The fault of these plays lies in the very exaltation of their tone. They are unnatural. They are artificial, with a form which many men in many decades have felt was improperly imposed upon them from the French[12] as a result of the royal exile at the Parisian court.[13] Yet they have a merit all their own, a quaintness and a charm, an almost mechanical beauty. They are put together from numerous sources, but shaped in a new mold. In fact, the King was not far wrong telling those who charged Dryden with plagiarism "he only desired that they who accused Dryden of thefts would steal him plays like these." We close this brief praise of Dryden's plays, then, with quotation of a passage from *Aurengzebe* (1676), which has been praised by the author of the *Spectator* papers and by the thundering Dr. Johnson, who did not always approve of Dryden, and which certainly is *The Vanity of Human Wishes* or *Rasselas* in a nutshell:

> When I consider life, 'tis all a cheat;
> Yet, fooled with hope, men favour the deceit;
> Trust on, and think to-morrow will repay:
> To-morrow's falser than the former day;
> Lies worse, and, while it says, we shall be blest
> With some new joys, cuts off what we possesst.
> Strange cozenage! None would live past years again,
> Yet all hope pleasure in what yet remain;
> And, from the dregs of life, think to receive,
> What the first sprightly running could not give.
> I'm tired with waiting for this chemic gold,
> Which fools us young, and beggars us when old.

[12] A chance line, though in a character who is being ridiculed, may be quoted from *Marriage à la Mode* (1673): "I'd sacrifice my life for French poetry."

[13] It must be remembered that decent tradesmen, professional men and bankers could not be seen at the theater—through prejudice—and that the audience was consequently chiefly aristocratic.

III

It was in the form of prefaces to these plays and others that Dryden published the prose writing which has entitled him to one of the most prominent places as a creator of modern English prose style.[14] Save for a very slight tendency toward the balanced construction—a tendency not nearly so outrageous as in Lyly and Sidney, in Bacon or Milton—we might easily mistake his for modern writing. There is ease and decision, and variety, too, in his paragraphs. There is wealth of well-rounded thought, not barely expressed, and sufficient quantity of allusion and quotation to lend richness and strength without too much encumbrance. He has read sufficiently to provide this detail, but he also provided a classical inclination. In the preface to *Troilus and Cressida* (1679) he found fault with earlier versions of the story because in them false Cressida went unpunished. This would never do. The old dramatic rules and regulations were as moral as they were strict, and Dryden meant to abide by the old rules and regulations. In the well-known *Essay of Dramatic Poesy* (1668) he defends the unities; in the preface to *The Mock Astrologer* (1671) he shows a reasonably wide knowledge of the drama, and on the basis of his study declares against extravagance in comedy and in tragedy; and in the preface to *Troilus and Cressida* he boasts—not without some condemnation of Shakespeare—that he has maintained due consideration for the unity of place and the proportion of time, and will have

---

[14] See W. E. Bolen, "Development of Dryden's Literary Criticism," *Publications of the Modern Language Association*, 1907, and "Dryden as a Prose Writer," *Catholic University Bulletin*, March, 1914.

"no leaping from Troy to the Grecian tent, and back again, in the same act." It is not surprising, therefore, to find him deploring Beaumont and Fletcher and praising Ben Jonson, who, he says, "is to be admired for many excellencies, and can be taxed with fewer failings than any English poet." Shakespeare he admired as a great genius who "had a universal mind" and criticized as a violator of laws of the stage.[15] He also adapted from him and was frank enough to say that where he imitated Shakespeare he excelled himself by so doing.[16] There is more in these estimates than Dryden's mere opinion; there is a shadow of the theory of his own art, for he himself said that the prefaces so laboriously written had instructed the public to a level where he could not attain. But Dryden firmly believed the Restoration age superior to that of Shakespeare; the master dramatist of Elizabethan drama was to him very nearly the same "great barbarian" as to the later eighteenth century:

"If Shakespeare were stripped of all the bombasts in his passions, and dressed in the most vulgar words, we should find the beauties of his thoughts remaining; if his embroideries were burnt down, there would still be silver at the bottom of the melting pot; but I fear (at least let me fear it for myself) that we, who ape his sounding words, have nothing of his thought, but are all outside; there is not so much as a dwarf within our giant's clothes. Therefore, let not Shakespeare suffer for our sakes; 'tis our fault,

---

[15] Preface to *Troilus and Cressida* (1679).
[16] Preface to *All for Love* (1678). Lyndaraxa in *The Conquest of Granada* (1672) is somewhat similar to Lady Macbeth, save in being ambitious only for herself. (See Part II, Act II, Scene 3.) In the same play is "a wood of lances and a moving war" and Macbeth is quoted in *Marriage à la Mode*.

who succeed him in an age which is more refined, if we imitate him so ill that we copy his failings only and make a virtue of that in our writings which in his was an imperfection."

Here is the dramatist turned critic, or—more significantly—the critic turned dramatist, and no man would agree more readily to condemn his own improprieties and barbarisms than Dryden himself. He who was one of the first to do anything like, to suggest anything like, a historical method of criticism, felt that his age inherited the virtues of past ages, the perfections of form, the niceties of expression and the niceties of moral endings. He considered this a great advantage, that he and his contemporaries lived in a time when the language, wit, and conversation were improved and refined over those of times that had gone before Dryden agreed that it is not unreasonable to expect their plays to derive some advantage from this general advancement. Certain it is that whatever may be said in detraction of his overrefined dramas,[17] his prose has richness and flavor that place it for all time among the best specimens of dramatic criticism in any language. The words of Dr. Johnson are as just as they are final:

"The criticism of Dryden is the criticism of a poet; not a dull collection of theorems, nor a rude detection of faults, which perhaps the censor was able to have committed, but a gay and vigorous dissertation, where delight is mingled with instruction and where the author proves his right of judgment by his power of performance. . . . With Dryden

[17] Congreve said: "We refine upon our pleasures." It was the spirit of the age.

we are wandering in quest of Truth, whom we find, if we find her at all, dressed in the graces of elegance, and if we miss her, the labor of the pursuit rewards itself; we are led only through fragrance and flowers."

What though they seem too much the flowers of the hothouse? Even in their artificiality they are exquisite.

# Bibliographies

## 1. CHAUCER

*The Student's Chaucer*, edited by W. W. Skeat (Oxford University Press, 1894).

Frederick Tupper, *Types of Society in Mediaeval Literature* (New York: Henry Holt & Company, 1926).

John Matthews Manly, *Some New Light on Chaucer* (Henry Holt & Company, 1926).

John Livingston Lowes, *Geoffrey Chaucer* (Houghton Mifflin Company, 1934).

G. K. Chesterton, *Chaucer* (New York: Farrar and Rinehart, 1932).

William George Dodd, *Courtly Love in Chaucer and Gower* (Boston: Ginn & Company, 1913).

Charles Sears Baldwin, *An Introduction to English Medieval Literature* (New York: Longmans, Green & Company, 1914).

*Canterbury Tales*, translated by Frank Ernest Hill (London: Longmans, Green & Company, 1930).

Geoffrey Chaucer, *Canterbury Tales*, rendered into Modern English by J. U. Nicolson (New York: Covici Fried, 1934).

George Lyman Kittredge, *Chaucer and His Poetry* (Cambridge: Harvard University Press, 1915).

Dean Spruill Fansler, *Chaucer and the Roman de la Rose* (New York: Columbia University Press, 1914).

George A. Plimpton, *The Education of Chaucer* (New York: Oxford University Press, 1935).

Sister M. Madeleva, *Pearl: A Study* (New York: D. Appleton & Company, 1925).

Bernhard Ten Brink, *The Language and Meter of Chaucer*,

translated by M. Bentinck Smith. Second Edition (London: The Macmillan Company, 1901).

Robert K. Root, "Publication Before Printing," in *Publications of the Modern Language Association of America*, 1913, Vol. XXVIII, pp. 417-431.

Ezra Kempton Maxfield, "Chaucer and Religious Reform," in *Publications of the Modern Language Association of America*, 1924, Vol. XXXIX, p. 74.

Frederick Tupper, "Chaucer and the Seven Deadly Sins," in *Publications of the Modern Language Association of America*, 1914, Vol. XXIX, pp. 96 ff.

Frederick Tupper, "Chaucer's Bed's Head," in *Modern Language Notes*, 1915, Vol. XXX, p. 7.

## 2. PIERS THE PLOWMAN

*A Mediaeval Anthology*, collected by Mary G. Segar (London: Longmans, Green & Company, 1915).

Frank Allen Patterson, *The Middle English Penitential Lyric* (New York: Columbia University Press, 1911).

Joseph A. Mosher, *The Exemplum in Early English Literature* (New York: Columbia University Press, 1911).

Sister M. Madeleva, *Pearl: A Study* (New York: D. Appleton & Company, 1925).

Rupert Taylor, *The Political Prophecy in England* (New York: Columbia University Press, 1911).

W. W. Skeat, *Piers the Plowman*, edited in three parallel texts (Oxford: Clarendon Press, 1886).

Jessie L. Weston, *Romance, Vision, and Satire* (Boston: Houghton Mifflin Company, 1912).

Joseph S. Tunison, *Dramatic Traditions of the Dark Ages* (Chicago: University of Chicago Press, 1907).

E. K. Chambers, *The Mediæval Stage* (Oxford: Clarendon Press, 1903).

## 3. JOHN HEYWOOD

Robert W. Bolwell, *The Life and Works of John Heywood* (New York: Columbia University Press, 1921).

Alfred W. Pollard, "John Heywood: Critical Essay," in Volume One, Charles Mills Gayley, *Representative English Comedies* (New York: The Macmillan Company, 1903).

F. W. Fairholt, "Some Account of John Heywood and His Interludes," in *Publications of the Percy Society*, Vol. XX.

Karl Young, "The Influence of French Farce upon John Heywood," in *Modern Philology*, 1904, Vol. II, pp. 97–124.

## 4. CHRISTOPHER MARLOWE

C. F. Tucker Brooke, *The Works of Christopher Marlowe* (Oxford: The Clarendon Press, 1910).

Havelock Ellis, *The Best Plays of Christopher Marlowe* (The Mermaid Series) (London: Fisher Unwin, 1887).

## 5. TWO ELIZABETHANS

John Erskine, *The Elizabethan Lyric* (New York: The Macmillan Company, 1903).

M. F. Crow, *Elizabethan Sonnet Cycles*, 1896–1898.

Alfred Noyes, *Tales of the Mermaid Tavern* (New York: Frederick A. Stokes Company, 1913).

Sidney Lee, "Elizabethan Sonnets" (2 vols.) in E. Arber, *The English Garner* (London: J. M. Dent & Company, 1903–4).

Sidney Lee, "Thomas Lodge," in *Dictionary of National Biography*.

R. Carl, "Ueber Thos. Lodge's Leben und Werks, Eine Kritische Untersuchung in Auschuss au David Laing," in *Anglia*, 1887, Vol. X, pp. 235–289.

L. E. Kastner, "Thomas Lodge as an Imitator of the Italian Poets," in *Modern Language Review*, 1906, Vol. II, pp. 155 ff.

Brinsley Nicholson and C. H. Herford, *The Best Plays of Ben Jonson* (The Mermaid Series), (London: Fisher Unwin, 1894).

Felix E. Schelling, "Ben Jonson and the Classical School," in *Publications of the Modern Language Association of America*, 1898, Vol. XIII, pp. 221 ff.

## 6–7. SHAKESPEARE

E. K. Chambers, *William Shakespeare* (Oxford: Clarendon Press, 1930).

W. A. Neilson and Ashley H. Thorndike, *The Facts about Shakespeare* (New York: The Macmillan Company, 1913).

Contain excellent bibliographies, to give mere extracts from which would be presumptuous. We find it only necessary to call attention to the few writings on Shakespeare's religion mentioned in the first footnote to the sixth chapter of this present book.

For those who may care to pursue this subject further, interest might be found in Sir Sidney Lee's description in the London *Times* of April 10, 1922 (Summarized in the *New York Times Book Review*, April 30, 1922) of the particular manner in which a local Spanish censor in 1645 expurgated certain passages from a copy of the Second Folio of 1632 destined for reading by young seminarians in the English College at Valladolid.

## 8. SOUTHWELL AND CRASHAW

John Erskine, *The Elizabethan Lyric* (New York: The Macmillan Company, 1903).

Jefferson B. Fletcher, *The Religion of Beauty in Woman* (New York: The Macmillan Company, 1911).

*The Poetical Works of the Rev. Robert Southwell*, edited by W. B. Turnbull (London: John Russell Smith, 1856).

*The Poetical and Prose Works of Robert Southwell*, edited by W. G. Walter, 2 vols. (London, 1828).

Pierre Janelle, *Robert Southwell the Writer* (London: Sheed and Ward, 1935).

Sister Rose Anita Morton, *An Appreciation of Robert Southwell* (Philadelphia: University of Pennsylvania Press, 1929).

Mario Praz, "Robert Southwell's 'St. Peter's Complaint' and its Source," in *The Modern Language Review*, 1924, Vol. XIX, pp. 273–290.

*The Complete Works of Richard Crashaw*, edited by W. B. Turnbull (London: John Russell Smith, 1858).

Richard Crashaw, *The Poems, English, Latin, and Greek*, edited by L. C. Martin (Oxford: Clarendon Press, 1927).

*Richard Crashaw, a Study in Style and Poetic Development*, by Ruth C. Wallerstein (Madison: University of Wisconsin Press, 1935).

## 9. THREE SEVENTEENTH-CENTURY DRAMATISTS

### Massinger

Arthur Symons, *The Best Plays of Philip Massinger* (London: Fisher Unwin, 1889).

Emil Koeppel's chapter on "Philip Massinger" in *Cambridge History of English Literature*, Vol. VI, pp. 160 ff., especially at pages 169–170.

### Shirley

Edmund Gosse, *The Best Plays of James Shirley* (London: Fisher Unwin, 1888).

Arthur H. Nason, *James Shirley* (New York: 1912).

Robert S. Forsythe, *The Relation of Shirley's Plays to the Elizabethan Drama* (New York: Columbia U. Press, 1915).

D'AVENANT

Killis Campbell, "Notes on D'Avenant's Life," in *Modern Language Notes*, 1903, Vol. XVIII, pp. 236 ff. The family tree in this is unreliable.

*Maid of Honour and the Siege of Rhodes*. By William D'Avenant. Edited by James W. Tupper (Boston: D. C. Heath & Co., 1909).

*The Dramatic Works of Sir William D'Avenant*. 5 vols. (Edinburgh: William Paterson, 1872-4).

Alfred Harbage, *Sir William Davenant, Poet Venturer, 1606-1668* (Philadelphia: University of Pennsylvania Press, 1935).

Alvin Thaler, "Thomas Heywood, D'Avenant, and the Siege of Rhodes," in *Publications of the Modern Language Association of America* (1924), Vol. XXXIX, pp. 624 ff.

10. DRYDEN

George Saintsbury, *Dryden* (English Men of Letters), (New York: Harper and Brothers, 1881).

Thomas B. Macaulay, "Dryden," in *The Miscellaneous Works of Lord Macaulay*, Vol. I, pp. 108-152 (New York: Harper and Brothers, n.d.).

James Russell Lowell, "Dryden," in *Among My Books*, pp. 1-80 (Boston: Houghton Mifflin and Company, 1870).

Christopher Hollis, *Dryden* (London: Duckworth & Co., 1933).

*The Works of John Dryden*, edited by George Saintsbury, 18 vols. (Edinburgh: William Patterson, 1882-1892).

Louis I. Brevold, *The Intellectual Milieu of John Dryden* (Ann Arbor: University of Michigan Press, 1934).

Mark Van Doren, *The Poetry of John Dryden* (New York: Harcourt, Brace and Howe, 1920).

Brother Leo, "Dryden as a Prose Writer," in *Catholic University Bulletin* (March, 1914), Vol. XX, pp. 211 ff.

# Index

*A Larum for London*, Lodge's, 79, 82
*Absalom and Achitophel*, Dryden's, 177; Settle and, 182
Addison, 73; on Dryden, 186
*Alarum Against Usurers*, Lodge's, 74
*Alchemist*, Johnson's, 85, 92, 94
*All for Love*, Dryden's, 188
*All's Well that Ends Well*, Shakespeare's, 132
Ambrose of Milan, 13, 21
*American Catholic Quarterly Review*, vi, xiii
Anti-clericalism, 33
Ariosto, Lodge and, 78
Aristotle, 62, 63, 67; tragedy of, 69
Arundel, Shakespeare's, 109
*As You Like It*, Shakespeare's, 88, 125, 129; Lodge and, 75
*Assignation*, Dryden's, 178
*Astræa Redux*, Dryden's, 176
Atkins, on Lodge, 73, 76
Augustine, St., 13, 21
*Aurengzebe*, Dryden's, 183, 186
Author, the, xii–xiii

Bacon, Francis, Dryden and, 187; Jonson and, 94; on Southwell, 149; quoted, 140
Baker, G. P., on Lodge, 81
Baldwin, C. S., on Chaucer, 6, 9; on Langland, 12
Ball, John, 26, 52, 54, 106
Baltimore, Lord, and D'Avenant, 166

Barabas, 61, 62, 65, 68, 69
*Bartholomew Fair*, Jonson's 92, 93
Beaufort, Goldwin Smith on, 111
Beaumont and Fletcher, 163, 183; Dryden on, 188
*Believe as You List*, Massinger's, 168, 171
Bembo, Lodge and, 78
Benson, Robert Hugh, 37; *Come Rack! Come Rope!* 122
Blakely, Father, quoted, 2
Blount, Charles, on Southwell, 145
Bobadill, Captain, 85
Boccaccio 4; Chaucer and, 6
Bolen, W. E., on Dryden, 187
Bolwell, Robert W., on Heywood, 47; cited, 58
*Book of the Duchess*, Chaucer's, 6, 8
Bowden, H. S., on Shakespeare, 97
Brooke, Rupert, quoted, 149
Brown, Thomas, on Dryden, 177
Browning, 68
Bullen, Shakespeare's, 115
Buckingham, Shakespeare's, 109, 116
Bunyan, *Pilgrim's Progress*, 38, 154
Burgess, William, on Shakespeare, 97, 121
*Burning Babe*, Southwell's, 93, 148, 152
Byron, 73; Crashaw and, 157, 158

Caedmon, 25; *Hymn to Christ*, 12
Campion, 143
*Canterbury Tales*, Chaucer's, 7–22
*Cardinal*, Shirley's, 159–160, 163–

197

164, 171
Carlisle, Bishop of, Shakespeare's, 109
Carlyle, 28; cited, 40
*Carmen Deo Nostro*, Crashaw's, 153
*Castel of Perseuerance*, 38
Catholic Literary Revival, ix, xii, xiii
Catholic literature, 22, 24–25, 30–31, 63
Catholicism, English, 113, 142; in literature, 68; in Shakespeare, 122–123; Lodge, 72; of Shakespeare, 47–117
Catullus, 142
Cavendish, 113
Caxton, 137
Cecil, Sir Robert, 113; on Southwell, 143
Chalmers on Heywood, 46
Chapman, Jonson and, 86
Character, depiction of, in Chaucer, 3, 9, 10, 14–15
Characters, dramatic, 98
Charles II, 176, 177, 180
Chaucer, ix, 89; a man of the world, 1, 2, 4–6; Baldwin on, 6, 9; biography, 3–5, 11; *Book of the Duchess*, 6, 8; *Canterbury Tales*, 7–22; Catholicism of, 1, 13–14; *Complaint of Mars*, 6; *Complaint of Venus*, 6; *Complaint to Pity*, 6; *Parliament of Birds*, 6; Dodd on, 9, 10; Dryden on, 1; depiction of character, 14–15; fame, xv, 1; *Franklin's Tale*, 7, 9–10, 11; Gower and, 16–17; Hazlitt on, 14–15; *House of Fame*, 7; indecency in, 15–16, 18, 22, 57; *Knight's Tale*, 8, 9; Langland and, 40; *Legend of Good Women*, 7; Lowes on, 4–5, 9, 15; *Man of Lawes Tale*, 17–18, 37; *Manciple's Tale*, 17–18; Manly on, 1, 6, 11; *Miller's Tale*, 15, 57; Nun's Priest, 13; *Nun's Priest's Tale*, 22; on Seven Deadly Sins, 16–19; *Pardoner's Tale*, 18, 22; Parson, 12; *Parson's Tale*, 16–19, 26–27, 36; *Physician's Tale*, 15, 18, 19–21; Prioress, 12; *Prioress's Tale*, 19–20; Reeve, 12; *Reeve's Tale*, 57; *Second Nun's Prologue*, 18; Shakespeare and, 14–15; storyteller, 33; *Summoner's Tale*, 18; translation by, Hill, F. E., 8, 15, 21–22; translation by MacKaye, Percy, 15; translation by Nicolson, J. U., 15; *Troilus and Cressida*, 7, 15; Tupper on, xv, 16–19, 21; *Wife of Bath's Tale*, 17–18
Chaucerian, pseudo, *Tale of Gamelyn*, 75
Chesterton, G. K., xii; cited, 170; on Langland, 23; quoted, 131
Chicheley, Shakespeare's, 109
Cicero, 6, 142; quoted, 82–83
Cinthio, Shakespeare's *Measure for Measure* and, 119
Clarke, C. C., on Shakespeare, 121
Classics, English, ix, xv
Coleridge, on drama, 118; on Jonson, 94
Colman, 171
Collier, J. P., on Dryden, 178; on Lodge, 81
*Come Rack! Come Rope!* Benson's, 122
Comedy, British, 168, 171; early, 58
*Comedy of Errors*, Shakespeare's, 124, 125
*Complaint of Mars*, Chaucer's, 6
*Complaint of Venus*, Chaucer's, 6
*Complaint to Pity*, Chaucer's, 6
Congreve, 171, 172; quoted, 189; on Dryden, 182; *Way of the World*, 186
*Conquest of Granada*, Dryden's,

# Index

179, 183, 184, 188
Contentment Is My Wealth, Lyly's, 65
Court of love, 7, 8, 9, 21
Courthope, cited, 139, 140
Cranmer, Shakespeare's, 115
Crashaw, Richard, biography, 152–153; Byron and, 158–159; *Carmen Deo Nostro*, 153; *Flaming Heart*, quoted, 156; Gosse on, 154, 157; Herbert and, 154; Moore, Tom, and, 158; Poe and, 157; Pope, Alexander, and, 158; religious banishment, xi; Shelley and, 154–155, 157–158; Shelling on, 155; Southwell and, 154; *Steps to the Temple*, 153; Swinburne and, 157
Cromwell, D'Avenant and, 166; Dryden and, 176, 177
Crow on Lodge, 78
Cumberland, 171
*Cynthia's Revels*, Jonson's, 88, 89

Daniel, 75
Dante, 4; Chaucer and, 6
D'Avenant, William, 160; Beaumont and Fletcher and, 168; Catholicism, xi; Cromwell and 166; dramas, 172; Dryden and, 167, 172, 183; Dryden successor to, 177–178; Harbage on, 166; loss of his nose, 180; *Love and Honour*, 172, 174, 175, 184; *News from Plymouth*, 168, 171; *Platonic Lovers*, 168, 171; religion, 166–167; *Siege of Rhodes*, 172–175, 183; *Wits*, 168, 171; work, 167–175
Defense of Poetry, Lodge's, 83
Defoe, 73
Dekker, 74; Jonson and, 88, 89; Massinger and, 161
*Description of a Most Noble Lady*, Heywood's, 50
Desportes, Lodge and, 78
*Devil Conjured*, Lodge's, 83

Dibdin, 171
*Discoveries*, Jonson's, 94
Dodd, W G., on Chaucer, 9, 10
Dowden, Edward on King John, 102; on Shakespeare's *Henry IV*, 106
*Dunciad*, Dryden in, 180
Drama, early, 56, 58; early Church, 24–25; Elizabethan, 61; heroic, 183 ff.; Jonson on, 87–88; Lodge's, 76
Drayton, 75; Jonson and, 84
*Drummond, Conversations with William*, 85
Dryden, John, ix, xv, 159; *Absalom and Achitophel*, 177; Addison on, 186; age of, 176; *All for Love*, 188; *Assignation*, 178; *Astræa Redux*, 176; *Aurengzebe*, 183, 186; Bacon and, 187, biography, 176–182; combative spirit of, 180; Bolen, W. E., on, 187; Brown, Thomas, on, 177; Collier, J. P., on, 178; Congreve on, 182; *Conquest of Granada*, 179, 183, 184, 188; Cromwell and, 176, 177; death of, 182; D'Avenant and, 167, 172, 183; D'Avenant, successor to, 177–178; *Dunciad* and, 180; *Essay of Dramatic Poesy*, 187; heroic drama and, 183; *Hind and the Panther*, 180; Howe, P. P., on, 182; James II and, 177; Johnson, Dr., on, 178, 186, 189; Jonson and, 94, 177; Lyly and, 187, Macaulay on, 178; *MacFlecknoe*, 180; *Marriage à la Mode*, 179, 188; *Medal*, 180; Milton and, 187; *Mock Astrologer*, 187; Nell Gwyn and, 184; on Beaumont and Fletcher, 188; on Jonson, Ben, 188; on Shirley, 171; plagiarism of, 186; Pope and, 180; prefaces of, 181; prose style of, 187; *Religio Laici*, 177, 179; religion of, 176–179; Root, R. K., on, 177, 178; Saintsbury on, 178, 181; Scott

on, 178; Settle, Elkanah, and, 180; Shadwell and, 180; on Shakespeare, 187–189; Sidney and, 187; *Spanish Friar*, 178; *Troilus and Cressida*, 187, 188; unities, dramatic, 187
Dudley, 113

*Eastward Hoe*, Jonson, Marston, and Chapman's, 86
*Ecclesiastical Review*, vi
Edward I, 105
Edward II, 105
Elizabeth, Queen, 48, 49, 70, 123, 143, 160
Elizabethan England, 70, 89 119, 168; Heywood on, 60; religion in, 98, 117
Elizabethan literature, 159; Jonson and, 94; Lodge and, 83
*Emblems*, Francis Quarles's, 154
England, Catholic, xv, 1, 2, 12, 24, 30, 97; Elizabethan, 70, 89, 119, 168
*Essay of Dramatic Poesy*, Dryden's, 187
*Euphues*, Lodge's, 76; Lyly's, 138, 140
*Euphues' Shadow*, Lodge's, 76
Euphuists, 88, 146
*Every Man in His Humour*, Jonson's, 79, 88, 89, 93, 94

*Facts About Shakespeare*, 99
Falstaff, 40, 106, 108; Bobadill and, 85; Shakespeare's, 127
Farmer, John S., on Heywood, 47
*Fatal Dowry*, Massinger's, 171
*Faustus, Dr.*, Marlowe's, 61, 62, 64, 65, 68, 69; quoted, 138, 139
Fitzwilliam, 114
*Flaming Heart*, Crashaw's, quoted, 156
Fletcher, 172, 173; morality, 170; Shakespeare and, 112
Forsythe, on Massinger and Shirley, 162; on Shirley, 170

Foster, 171
*Foure PP*, Heywood's, 53, 57
Furnivall on Shakespeare, 131–132
*Franklin's Tale*, Chaucer's, 7, 9–10, 11
French literature, 6, 7, 8, 26, 78, 137–138
Friars, in Shakespeare, 130

*Game of Chess*, Heywood's, 163
*Gamester*, Shirley's, 168
Garnett, Dr., quoted, 140
*Gentleness and Nobility*, Heywood's, 53, 54, 59
Gervinus, G. G., on Shakespeare, 107
*Gesta Romanorum*, 39
*Ghyrland of the Blessed Virgin*, Jonson's, 93
Gibbins, H. de B., cited, 41, 52, 113
Gloster, Shakespeare's, 111
Gosse, Edmund, on Crashaw, 154, 157; on Lodge, 72, 82; on Shirley, 159–160, 163, 171
Gosson, Lodge on, 73, 74; *School of Abuse*, 73
Gower, 3; Chaucer and, 8, 16–17
Greene, Robert, 76; Lodge and, 79; Shakespeare and, 128; Shakespeare's *Winter's Tale* and, 119
Grey, 113
*Guardian*, Massinger's, 160, 170
*Gull's Horn Book*, 89
Gwyn, Nell, and Dryden, 184

Halévy, Ludovic, 87
*Hamlet*, Shakespeare's, 104–105, 107, 118, 122, 125, 132; discussed, 134–136; Schlegel on, 34
Harbage, Alfred, on D'Avenant, 166
Hazlitt, William, on Chaucer, 14–15
Heine on Puritanism, 123
Henley, William Ernest, quoted, 184
Henrietta Maria, Queen, xi, 162

# Index

Henry III, 105
Henry IV, Shakespeare's, 106, 109–112; date of, 99; Dowden on, 106
Henry V, Shakespeare's, 106, 107, 118; date of, 99
Henry VI, Shakespeare's, 106, 108, 117; date of, 99
Henry VIII, 32, 45, 46, 48, 49, 142
Henry VIII, Shakespeare's, 85; date of, 99; *King John* and, 116; Smith, Goldwin, on, 114; Walsh on, 112
Herbert, George, 114, 139; Crashaw and, 154
Herford on Jonson, 88, 91–92
Herrick, Robert, 139
Heywood, John, biography, 45, 46–49; Bolwell on, cited, 58; Catholicism, 47, 48; Chalmers on, 46; *Description of a Most Noble Lady*, 50; dramatic writings, 55; *Foure PP*, 53, 57; *Gentleness and Nobility*, 53, 54, 59; Langland and, 57, on Elizabethan England, 60; *Play of the Wether*, 58; Pollard on, 58; *Spider and the Flie*, 49, 51, 53, 54, 59; *Wit and Folly*, 53; *Workes*, 49
Heywood, Thomas, *Game of Chess*, 163; morality, 170
Hill, Frank Ernest, translation of Chaucer, 8, 15, 21–22
*Hind and the Panther*, Dryden's, 180
Historical drama, Shakespeare's, 117
*Hieronimo Is Mad Again!*, 88
Holbach, 35, 36
Holinshed, Shakespeare and, 118
Homer, 142
Horace, Jonson and, 94, 139
Horne, Richard Hengist, on Marlowe, 66–67
Hotson, Leslie, on Marlowe, 63
*House of Fame*, Chaucer's, 7
Howe, P. P., on Dryden, 182
*Hyde Park*, Shirley's, 168

*Hymn to Christ*, Caedmon's, 12

Indecency, in Chaucer, 15–16, 18, 22, 57
*Infans et Mundus*, 39
*Invictus*, Henley's, quoted, 184
Ireland, Shirley and, 164–165
Italian literature, 4, 7, 78, 89, 119, 137–138

James I, 159; Jonson and, 90
James II, 164; Dryden and, 177; Scott on, 180
Jameson, Mrs., on Shakespeare, 132, 133–134
Janelle, on Southwell, 144
Jerome, 13, 21
*Jew of Malta*, Marlowe's, 61, 62, 65, 68, 69
Joan of Arc, Shakespeare on, 117
Johnson, Dr. Samuel, 46, 84; cited, 139; on Aurengzebe, 186; on Dryden, 177, 178, 186, 189
Jones, Inigo, Jonson and, 86
Jonson, Ben, a soldier, 85; Ajax in *Troilus and Cressida*, 89; *Alchemist*, 85, 92, 94; Bacon and, 94; *Bartholomew Fair*, 92, 93; biography, 70–71, 84–91; British comedy, 171; Catholicism, x–xi, 85, 91–92; classicism, 94; Coleridge on, 94; criticism and, 88; *Cynthia's Revels*, 88, 89; Dekker and, 88; *Discoveries*, 94; Dryden on, 94, 188; Euphuists, and, 88; *Every Man Out of His Humour*, 79, 85, 88, 89 93, 94; *Ghyrland of the Blessed Virgin*, 93; Herford on, 88, 91–92; Horace and, 139; James I, and, 90; Jones, Inigo, and, 86; love, definition of, 185; Marston and, 86, 88; Martial and, 139; Massinger and, 159, 168, 169, 170; nationalism, 89; pastoral poetry and, 88; plays of, 87; quoted, 139; on poetry, 88, 95; on poverty, 95;

## 202  Index

*Poetaster*, 88; *Sejanus*, 91, 93; on Southwell, 146; Pembroke, Earl of, and, 90; Shakespeare and 85, 94; *Silent Woman*, 94, 168; Southwell and, 93; successors, 167–168, 169; Swinburne on, 94; *Tale of a Tub*, 92; translated Horace, 94; translated Martial, 94; Vauclain, Lord, and, 94; Vergil, and, 139; *Volpone or the Fox*, 88, 93
*Julius Caesar*, Shakespeare's, 104, 118

*Katharine*, Shakespeare's, 114, 116
Keats quoted, 84
Kildare, Earl of, 164
King John, Goldwin Smith on, 99–100
*King John*, Shakespeare's, 97, 99–104; Dowden on, 102; Henry VIII and, 116
*King John, The Troublesome Reign of*, 100
Kingsley, on Shirley, 163
Knight, Chaucer's, 14
Knight, on Shakespeare, 123, 124
*Knight's Tale*, Chaucer's, 8, 9
Kyd, Shakespeare and, 128

Lamb, Charles, cited, 181
Langland, William, 3, 23–26, 89; a reformer, 41; Baldwin on, 12; Catholicism 34, 35; Chaucer and, 40; Chesterton on, 23; Heywood and, 53, 57; Manly on, 23–24, 31; Protestantism and, 23, 37–38; Shirley and, 164; Wiclif and, 39
Layamon, 25
*Lear*, Shakespeare's, 118, 135
Lee, Sir Sidney, on Lodge, 78; on Shakespeare's sonnets, 121
*Legend of Good Women*, Chaucer's, 7
*Life and Death of William Longbeard*, Lodge's, 76, 82
Literature, Catholic, xv, 2; Elizabethan, 73; Lodge on, 74

Lodge, Thomas, a doctor, 81; *A Larum for London*, 79, 82; *Alarum Against Usurers*, 74; Atkins on, 73; Baker, G. P., on, 81; biography, 70–71, 72–84; Catholicism, 82–83; Collier, J. P., on, 81; Crow on, 78; *Defense of Poetry*, 83; *Devil Conjured*, 83; dramas, 76; *Euphues' Shadow*, 76; Gosse on, 72; Jonson and, 84, 88; Lee, Sir Sidney, on, 78; *Life and Death of William Longbeard*, 76, 82; *Life of Robin the Devil*, 82; *Looking-glass for London and England*, 76, 79, 80; Lyly and, 76; Marlowe and, 80; on literature, 74; *Phillis*, 76–78; plagiarism, 78; *Poor Man's Talent*, 83; *Prosopoeia*, 83; *Rosalynde*, 75, 76; *Scilla's Metamorphosis*, 75, 79; sea scenes in, 76–78, 81; Shakespeare and, 75, 128; Walsingham, Sir Francis, and, 83; wife of, 83; *Wit's Misery*, 83; *Wounds of Civil War*, 76, 79, 80
Lollards, 106
*Looking-glass for London and England*, Lodge's, 76, 79, 80
*Love and Honour*, D'Avenant's, 172, 174, 175, 184
*Love's Labours Lost*, Shakespeare's, 126, 135
Lowes, J. L., on Chaucer, 4–5, 9
Lyly, *Contentment Is My Wealth*, 65; Dryden and, 187; *Euphues*, 76, 138, 140; Jonson and, 84; Lodge and, 76

Macaulay, on Dryden, 178
*Macbeth*, Shakespeare's, 118, 135; Dryden quoted, 188
*MacFlecknoe*, Dryden's, 180
Macklin, 171
Magna Carta, 101, 104
Malory, 89
*Man of Lawe's Tale*, Chaucer's, 17–18, 37

## Index

Manciple's Tale, Chaucer's, 17–18
Manly, on Chaucer, 1, 6, 11; on Langland, 23–24, 31
Manuscripts, 5, 23, 24, 27–28, 137
Marino, 138
Marlowe, 160; atheism, 10; biography, 61, 63; Catholicism, 63; *Dr. Faustus*, 61, 62, 64, 65, 68, 69; quoted, 138, 139; *Edward II*, 105; Horne, Richard Hengist, on, 66–67; Hotson Leslie, on, 63; *Jew of Malta*, 62, 65, 68, 69; Jonson and, 84; Lodge and, 80, 81; Noyes on, 66–67; *Richard III*, Shakespeare's, and, 118; Symons on, 171; *Tamburlaine*, 62, 65, 68, 69
*Marlowe*, Josephine Prescott Peabody's, 66–67
*Marriage à la Mode*, Dryden's, 179, 186, 188
Marston, Jonson and, 86, 88
Martial, Jonson and, 94, 139
*Mary Magdalen's Complaint*, Southwell's, 151
Mary Stuart, John Heywood and, 48, 50, 51
Matthews, Brander, on Massinger, 161
MacKaye, P., translation of Chaucer, 15
Maxfield, E. K., on Chaucer, 13–14
*Menechini*, Plautus's, 124
*Measure for Measure*, Shakespeare's, 122, 124, 131, 132; Cinthio and, 119
*Medal*, Dryden's, 180; Settle and, 182
Menander, Shakespeare and, 124
*Merchant of Venice*, Shakespeare's, 121, 125, 126, 135; quoted, 139
Mermaid Tavern, 71, 84–85, 160
Metaphysical poets, the, 139–140
Mézières, on Shakespeare, 120
Middleton, *A Trick to Catch the Old One*, 168; *Believe as You List*, 168, 171; Dekker and, 161; *Fatal Dowry*, 171; Forsythe on, 162; *Guardian*, 160, 171; Jonson and, 168, 169, 170; Matthews, Brander, on, 161; morality, 170; *New Way to Pay Old Debts*, 168; religion, 161–162; *Renegade*, 161; *Roman Actor*, 169; Symons on, 171; *Virgin Martyr*, 161
*Midsummer Night's Dream*, Shakespeare's, 132
*Miller's Tale*, Chaucer's, 15, 57
Milton, xi, 159; Dryden and, 187; *Paradise Lost*, 154
*Mock Astrologer*, Dryden's, 187
Monasteries, dissolution of, 112–113
Monks, Shakespeare's, 122 ff.
More, Sir Thomas, 46, 47, 48, 52, 53, 54, 57, 58, 89, 101; Shakespeare and, 112, 115
Morton, Sister Rose, on Southwell, 142
Moore, Tom, Crashaw and, 158
*Much Ado About Nothing*, Shakespeare's, 120, 122, 130

Nason, Arthur, on Shirley, 162
Nationalism, English, 100; Jonson's, 89
Nazianzus, Gregory, 142
*New Prince, New Pomp*, Southwell's, 151
*New Way to Pay Old Debts*, Massinger's, 168
Newman, xii, 32; opinions of, 178
*News from Plymouth*, D'Avenant's 168, 171
Nicolson, J. U., translation of Chaucer, 15
Norfolk, Shakespeare on, 108
Noyes, Alfred, on Marlowe, 66–67; *Tales of the Mermaid Tavern*, 66, 71, 84–85, 160
Nuns in Shakespeare, 132 ff.
Nun's Priest, Chaucer's, 13
*Nun's Priest's Tale*, Chaucer's, 22

Ogilby, bookseller, 181
*Old Wive's Tale*, 89
Orinda, the matchless, 164
*Orphan*, Otway's, 184
*Othello*, Shakespeare's, 125, 135
Otway, Thomas, *Orphan*, 184; *Venice Preserved*, 183
Ovid, 6, 142

Pandulph, 102–104
*Paradise Lost*, Milton's, 154
*Pardoner's, Tale*, Chaucer's, 18, 22
*Parliament of Birds*, Chaucer's, 6
Parson, Chaucer's, 12, 14, 16, 26–27
*Parson's Tale*, Chaucer's, 16–19, 36
Paschale, Lodge and, 78
Pastoral poetry, 88
Peabody, Josephine Prescott, on Marlowe, 66–67
Peale, Jonson and, 84
Peasant's Revolt, 106
Peele, Shakespeare and, 128
Pembroke, Earl of, 90; Massinger and, 161
Penance, Shakespeare on, 124
Percy, *Reliques*, 94, 127
*Pericles*, Shakespeare's, 125, 132
Petrarch, 4, 138; Lodge and, 78
*Phillis*, Lodge's, 76–78
*Physician's Tale*, Chaucer's, 15, 18, 19–21
*Piers Plowman*, form of, 23–24; Skeat on, 29, 32–33; text of, 27–28
Pilgrimage of Grace, 52, 113
*Pilgrim's Progress*, Bunyan's, 38, 154
Plato, 142
*Platonic Lovers*, D'Avenant's, 168, 171
*Play of the Wether*, Heywood's, 58
Plutarch, 79; Shakespeare and, 118, 124
Poe, Crashaw and, 157
*Poetaster*, Jonson's, 88

Poetry, Jonson on, 88, 94
Pollard, on Heywood, 58
*Poor Man's Talent*, Lodge's, 83
Pope, Alexander, 140, 152; Crashaw and, 158; Dryden and, 180
Printing, mechanical, 137
Prioress, Chaucer's, 12
*Prioress's Tale*, Chaucer's, 19–20
*Prosopoeia*, Lodge's, 83
Protestant Revolt, 65
Protestantism, 32, 52, 178; drama and, 104; English drama and, 100–101; Langland and, 37–38; Shakespeare and, 106; support of, 113–114
Puritanism, 74, 92; Heine on, 123; theatre and, 183

Quarles, *Emblems*, 154

Raich, J. M., on Shakespeare, 97
*Rasselas*, Johnson's, 186
Rastells, 47
Reeve, Chaucer's, 12
*Reeve's Tale*, Chaucer's, 57
Reform, 41
*Religio Laici*, Dryden's, 177, 179
Religious poetry, 29, 152
*Reliques*, Percy's, 127
Renaissance, 137
*Renegade*, Massinger's, 161
Restoration, 176; drama of, 182
Restoration drama, 172; Dryden on, 188
Restoration literature, 159
Rich, 114
*Richard II*, Shakespeare's, 104, 105–109; date of, 99
*Richard III*, Shakespeare's, 61, 106; date of, 99; Marlowe and, 118
*Rerum Novarum*, Leo XIII's, 43
*Robin the Devil, Life of*, Lodge's, 82
Robinson, James Harvey, 32
Roland, Madame, 65
*Roman Actor*, Massinger's, 169

## Index

Roman de la Rose, 38
Romanticism, 64–67
Rome, English College at, 142
*Romeo and Juliet*, Shakespeare's, 97, 122, 124, 125, 135
Ronsard, Lodge and, 78
Rosary, and Shakespeare, 123
*Rosalynde*, Lodge's, 75, 76; songs in, 77
Root, R. K., on Dryden, 177, 178
Roper, William, 47; *Life of More*, cited, 101
Runnymede, 101
Russell, 113
Russell, E. R., on Shakespeare, 97

St. Basil, 142
St. Chrysostom, 142
*St. Patrick for Ireland*, Shirley's, 164
*St. Peter's Complaint*, Southwell's, 149–150
Saintsbury, on Dryden, 178, 181
Sanazzara, Lodge and, 78
Schelling, Felix, on Crashaw, 155; on Southwell, 146
Schlegel, on Shakespeare, 122, 131; on Shakespeare's *Hamlet*, 134
Scholarship, 3, 8, 19, 63; fruits of, 120, uses of, 46–47
*School of Abuse*, Gosson's, 73
*Scilla's Metamorphosis*, Lodge's, 74, 79
Scott, Walter, individualism, 67, 68; on Charles II, 180; on Dryden, 178; on James II, 180; on King William, 180
Scrope, Shakespeare's, 109, 110
Second Nun, Chaucer's, 18
Seeger, Alan, quoted, 149
Segar, Mary, 2
*Sejanus*, Jonson's, 91, 93
Seneca, 61
Settle, Elkanah, death of, 182; Dryden and, 180, 182
Seven Deadly Sins, 16 ff.; Langland and, 34, 44
Seymour, 113
Shadwell, Dryden and, 180
Shakespeare, William, 159, 160; Abbot of Westminster, 109, 111, 115; *All's Well That Ends Well*, 132; Archbishop of York, 109; Arundel, 109; *As You Like It*, 88, 125, 129; *As You Like It*, and Lodge, 75; Beaufort, his, 111; Bishop of Carlisle, his, 109; Bowden on, 97; Buckingham, 109, 116; Bullen, 115; Burgess, William, on, 97, 121; Catholicism, ix–x, 97–117, 122–123; Chaucer and, 14–15; Chicheley, 109; Clarke, C. C., on, 121; *Comedy of Errors*, 124, 125; Cranmer, 115; Dowden on, 106; Dryden on, 187–189; Falstaff, 106, 108, 127; Fletcher and, 112; Friars in, 130; Furnivall on, 131–132; Gervinus on, 107; Gloster, 111; Greene and, 128; *Hamlet*, 104–105, 107, 118, 122, 125; *Hamlet* discussed, 134–136; *Hamlet*, nunnery in, 132; *Henry IV*, date of, 99; *Henry IV*, discussed, 106, 109–112; *Henry V*, date of, 99; *Henry V*, discussed, 106–107; *Henry VI*, 117; *Henry VI*, date of, 99; *Henry VI*, discussed, 106–108; *Henry VIII*, date of, 99; *Henry VIII* and *King John*, 116; Heywood, John, and, 46; historical drama, 117; Holinshed and, 118; Jameson, Mrs., on, 132, 133–134; Jonson and, 85, 94; *Julius Caesar*, 104, 118; Katharine, 114, 116; *King John* 97, 99–104; *King John*, Dowden on, 102; *King John*, Thorndike on, 100; *King John* and *Henry VIII*, 116; Knight on, 123, 124; Kyd and, 128; *Lear*, 118, 135; Lee, Sidney, on, 121;

Lodge and, 73, 75 128; *Love's Labours Lost*, 126, 135; *Macbeth*, 118, 135; marriage in, 129 ff.; *Measure for Measure*, 122, 124, 131, 132; *Measure for Measure* and Cinthio, 119; Menander and, 124; *Merchant of Venice*, 121, 125, 126, 135, 139; Mézières on, 120; *Midsummer Night's Dream*, 132; monks in, 122 ff.; *Much Ado About Nothing*, 120–122, 130; nuns in, 132 ff.; on Joan of Arc, 117; on Norfolk, 108; on Penance, 124; *Othello*, 125, 135; Peele and, 128; *Pericles*, 125, 132; Plautus and, 124; Plutarch and, 79, 118; predecessors of, 79; Raich, J. M., on, 97; religion of, 97; *Richard II*, cited, 104; *Richard II*, date of, 99; *Richard II*, discussed, 105–109; *Richard III*, 61, 106; *Richard III*, and Marlowe, 118; *Richard III*, date of, 99; *Romeo and Juliet*, 97, 122, 124, 125, 135; rosary and, 123; Russell on, 97; Schlegel on, 122, 131; Schlegel on *Hamlet*, 134; simplicity of, 138; sonnets, 121, 138, *Taming of the Shrew*, 127, 128; Tatlock on, 133; Thomas More, Sir, and, 112, 115; Thorndike on, 100; Thurston on, 97; *Titus Andronicus*, 128; *Troilus and Cressida*, Ben Jonson as Ajax in, 89; trumpets in, 183; *Twelfth Night*, 129; *Two Gentlemen of Verona*, 119, 122, 123, 124; *Venus and Adonis*, 132; Wallace on, 120; Walsh, J. J., on, 97; *Winter's Tale*, and Greene, 119; Wolsey, 111–112, 115–116

Shaw, G. B., long prefaces, 181

Shelley, 152; Crashaw and, 154–155, 157–158

Shirley, *A Witty Fair One*, 168; *Cardinal*, 159–160, 163–164, 170; Dryden on, 171, Forsythe, R. S., on, 170; *Gamester*, 168; Gosse, Edmund on, 160, 163; *Hyde Park*, 168; intrigues in, 183; Ireland and, 164–165; Kildare, Earl of, and, 164; Kingsley on, 163; Langland and, 164; morality, 170; Nason on, 162; religion, 162–166; *St. Patrick for Ireland*, 164; translations of, 181; Ward on, 163; Wood, Anthony à, on, 170

Sidney, Sir Philip, 73, 113, 146, 161; Dryden and, 187

*Siege of Rhodes*, D'Avenant's, 172–175, 183

*Silent Woman*, Johnson's, 94, 168

Sin, x

Skeat, W. W., on *Piers Plowman*, 29, 32–33

Smith, Goldwin, on Beaufort, 111; on dissolution of the monasteries, 113; on Henry VIII, 114; on King John, 99–100; on Scrope, 110; quoted, 106

*Soldiers, To True*, Jonson's, 86

Sonnets, Shakespeare's, 121, 138

Soul, Christian, 135

Southey, 73

Southwell, Robert, xv; Bacon on, 149; biography, 141–145; Blount on, 145; *Burning Babe*, 93, 152; *Burning Babe*, quoted, 148; Cecil, Sir Robert, on, 143; Crashaw and, 154; Janelle on, 144; Jonson and, 93, 146; martyrdom, 125; *Mary Magdalen's Complaint*, 151; *New Prince, New Pomp*, 151; *St. Peter's Complaint*, 149–150; Schelling on, 146; Sister Rose Morton on, 142; Thurston, 141; Topcliffe on, 143

*Spanish Friar*, Dryden's, 178

Spenser, 82, 160

# Index

Spider and the Flie, Heywood's, 49, 51, 53, 59
Steps to the Temple, Crashaw's, 153
Suckling, 139
Summoner, Chaucer's, 14
Summoner's Tale, Chaucer's, 18
Supremacy, Act of, 112
Swinburne, 68; Crashaw and, 157; on Jonson, 94
Symons, Arthur, on Marlowe, 171; on Massinger, 171

Tagore, 68
Tale of a Tub, Jonson's, 92
Tale of Gamelyn, pseudo-Chaucerian, 75
Tales of the Mermaid Tavern, Noyes's, 66–67, 71, 84–85, 160
Tamburlaine the Great, Marlowe's, 62, 65, 68, 69
Taming of the Shrew, Shakespeare's, 127–128
Tatlock, Prof. J. S. P., on Shakespeare, 133
Taylor, Rupert, cited, 30
Tempest, adaptation of, 183
Ten Commandments, 35; Langland and, 43
Tennyson, 68
Tennyson, quoted, 149
Thorndike, on Shakespeare's King John, 100
Thought, vi, xiii
Thurston, Herbert, on Shakespeare, 97; on Southwell, 141
Tibullus, 142
Tichborne, Chidiock, quoted, 146
Titus Andronicus, Shakespeare's, 128
Topcliffe, 143
Tottel's Miscellany, 50, 137
Tragedy, 21, 62; character of, 40
Trevelyan, G. M., cited, 34, 35
Trick to Catch the Old One, Middleton's, 168
Troilus and Cressida, Chaucer's, 7, 9, 15, 187, 188; Ben Jonson as Ajax in, 89
Troublesome Reign of King John, 100
Tunnyng of Eleanor Runnyng, 40
Tupper, Frederick, xv; on Chaucer, 16–19, 21
Twelfth Night, Shakespeare's, 129
Two Gentlemen of Verona, Shakespeare's, 119, 122, 123, 124, 125

United Kingdom, Goldwin Smith's, 100
Unities, dramatic, 87

Vanity and Human Wishes, Johnson's, 186
Vauclain, Jonson and, 94
Venice Preserved, Otway's, 183
Venus and Adonis, Shakespeare's, 132
Vergil, Jonson and, 139; quoted, 121; Southwell and, 142
Vicar of Bray, 45–46, 55
Villon, quoted, 138
Virgin Martyr, Massinger's, 161
Volpone or the Fox, Jonson's, 88, 93
Vulgate, 13

Wallace, on Shakespeare, 120
Walsh, James J., on Henry VIII, 112; on Shakespeare, 97
Walsingham, Sir Francis, Lodge and, 83
Ward, A. W., cited, 162; on Shirley, 163; quoted, 163
Ward, Robert, xvi
Wat Tyler's rebellion, 106
Way of the World, Congreve's, 176
Westminster, Abbot of, Shake-

speare's, 109, 111, 115
Whitman, 65; cited, 149
Wiclif, 13, 33, 105; Langland and, 39
*Wife of Bath's Tale*, Chaucer's, 17–18
William, King, Scott on, 180
*Winter's Tale*, Shakespeare's, and Greene, 119
Wit, definition of, 140
*Wit and Folly*, Heywood's, 53
*Wits*, D'Avenant's, 168, 171
*Wit's Misery*, Lodge's, 83
*Witty Fair One*, Shirley's, 168

Wolsey, Shakespeare's, 111–112, 115–116
Wood, Anthony à, D'Avenant and, 166; on Shirley, 170
Wordsworth, individualism, 67, 68; quoted, 149
*Wounds of Civil War*, Lodge's, 76, 79, 80
Wycherly, 171

York, Archbishop of, Shakespeare's, 109

Zenocrate, 62